Michael M. Dediu

Sutherland to Pavarotti:
Great Singers History

A chronological and photographic documentary

DERC Publishing House
Tewksbury (Boston), Massachusetts, U. S. A.

Copyright ©2019 by Michael M. Dediu

All rights reserved

Published and printed in the
United States of America
On the Great Seal of the United States are included:
E Pluribus Unum (Out of many, one)
Annuit Coeptis (He has approved of the undertakings)
Novus Ordo Seclorum (New order of the ages)

Library of Congress Control Number: 2019905160

Dediu, Michael M.

Sutherland to Pavarotti: Great Singers History
A chronological and photographic documentary

ISBN-13: 978-1-939757-89-0

Preface

It is well known that without good music, life would be a mistake, how a great philosopher once said. And that good music must be performed by really talented singers. Starting over 400 years ago, opera singers were always admired for their interpretations, which generate deep emptions, because, as Plato said, "Music is the movement of sound to reach the soul for the education of its virtue."

Great composers, from Giovanni Pierluigi da Palestrina, and Claudio Monteverdi, to Antonio Vivaldi, Johann Sebastian Bach, Wolfgang Amadeus Mozart and Giuseppe Verdi, just to name a few, created well-known compositions, and the famous opera singers, from La Florinda and Adamonti, to Adelina Patti, Nellie Melba, Chaliapin and Caruso, and to Amelita Galli-Curci, Dietrich Fischer-Dieskau, Joan Sutherland and Pavarotti, just to name a few, bring to life those magnificent compositions.

Using a chronological order, this book has a variety of relevant information not only about them, but also about numerous other personalities and important events. There are also many attractive and historic photographs, which add another visual dimension. The more you read, the more you'll love it!

This book brings a rainbow of artistical information, from many places and personalities, and all this information will certainly enhance everybody's joie de vivre. I want to thank my wife Sophia for her photo assistance.

These opera singers are part of our culture, and any reader, from everywhere, will definitely find, in this book of general interest, plenty of useful information, which will help them to better understand our history, and prepare them for a better future.

Michael M. Dediu, Ph. D.

Tewksbury (Boston), U. S. A., 23 May 2019

London, UK: From the Bow Street, the northeast façade of the Royal Opera House at Covent Garden (1732, 1808, 1858, 1999, capacity 2,256). In 1734, Covent Garden presented its first ballet, Pygmalion. On 14 January 1947, the Covent Garden Opera Company gave its first performance of Carmen (1875, opera in four acts, based on a novella of the same title by Prosper Mérimée (1803-1870 (age 67))) by French composer Georges Bizet (1838-1875 (age 36)).

Table of Contents

Preface 3
Table of Contents 5
Beginning of European music: 321 – 1583 9
    Guido d'Arezzo: 991 – 1033, 42 9
    Giovanni Pierluigi da Palestrina: 1525 – 1594, 69 10
    Jacopo Peri: 1561 – 1633, 71 10
    Claudio Monteverdi: 1567 – 1643, 76 10
Virginia Ramponi-Andreini: 1583 – 1630, 47 12
    Caterina Martinelli: 1589 – 1608, 19 12
    Odoardo Ceccarelli: 1600 – 1668, 68 12
Anna Renzi: 1620 – 1661, 41 13
    Margarita Salicola: 1659 – 1706, 47 13
    Demoiselle Conradi: 1660 – 1720, 60 14
    Francesca Margherita de l'Épine: 1680 – 1746, 66 15
    Anna Tessieri Girò: 1710 – 1750, 40 20
Valentin Adamberger (Adamonti): 1740 – 1804, 64 28
    Ludwig Fischer: 1745 – 1825, 79 30
    Francesco Benucci: 1745 – 1824, 79 31
    Emanuel Schikaneder: 1751 – 1812, 61 35
    Luísa Rosa de Aguiar Todi: 1753 – 1833, 80 36

Josefína Dušková (Josepha Duschek): 1754 – 1824, 70 37
   Adriana Ferrarese del Bene: 1755 – 1804, 49 37
   Caterina Magdalena Cavalieri: 1755 – 1801, 46 38
   Benedikt Emanuel Schack: 1758 – 1826, 68 39
   Salomea Deszner: 1759 – 1806, 47 40
Maria Aloysia Antonia Weber Lange: 1760 – 1839, 79 41
   Christine Rakhmanov: 1760 – 1827, 67 41
   Michael Kelly: 1762 – 1826, 63 42
   Teresa Saporiti-Codecasa: 1763 – 1869, 106 42
   Anna Maria Crouch: 1763 – 1805, 42 43
Anna Selina Storace (Nancy Storace): 1765 – 1817, 51 44
   Sofia Ulrika Liljegren (Sofia Uttini): 1765 - 1795, 30 45
   Luigi Bassi: 1766 – 1825, 59 46
   Jean Baptiste Édouard Louis Camille Du Puy: 1770 – 1822, 52 47
   Margareta Sofia Lagerqvist: 1771 – 1800, 29 48
   Anna Gottlieb: 1774 – 1856, 81 48
   Maria Malibran: 1808 – 1836, 28 55
Giorgio Ronconi: 1810 – 1890, 79 57
   Giuseppina Strepponi: 1815 – 1897, 82 58
   Leone Giraldoni: 1824 – 1897, 73 59
   Carlo Negrini: 1826 – 1865, 38 60
   Francesco Graziani: 1828 – 1901, 73 61
Antonio Cotogni: 1831 – 1918, 87 63
   Ernesto Nicolini: 1834 – 1898, 63 64
   Charles Santley: 1834 -1922, 88 65
Teresa Stolz: 1834 – 1902, 68 67

Adelina Patti: 1843 – 1919, 76 71

   Lilli Lehmann: 1848 – 1929, 80 76

   Sofia Scalchi: 1850 – 1922, 71 78

   Hariclea Darclée: 1860 – 1939, 78 86

Nellie Melba: 1861 – 1931, 69 88

   Eugenio Giraldoni: 1871 – 1924, 53 91

Feodor Chaliapin: 1873 – 1938, 65 94

Enrico Caruso: 1873 – 1921, 48 96

   Lalla Miranda: 1874 – 1944, 70 98

   Alice Geraldine Farrar: 1882 – 1967, 85 101

Amelita Galli-Curci: 1882 – 1963, 81 103

Beniamino Gigli: 1890 – 1957, 67 107

   Viorica Ursuleac: 1894 – 1985, 91 108

   Traian Grozăvescu: 1895 – 1927, 31 110

   Petre Ştefănescu Goangă: 1902 – 1973, 71 112

   Ion Dacian: 1911 – 1981, 70 113

Tito Gobbi: 1913 – 1984, 70 114

Mario Del Monaco: 1915 – 1982, 67 115

   Zenaida Pally: 1919 – 1997, 78 115

   Nicola Rossi-Lemeni: 1920 – 1991, 70 116

Giuseppe Di Stefano: 1921 – 2008, 86 118

Renata Tebaldi: 1922 – 2004, 82 119

Maria Callas: 1923 -1977, 53 121

   Elena Cernei: 1924 – 2000, 76 124

Dietrich Fischer-Dieskau: 1925 – 2012, 86 126

   Virginia Zeani: born 1925 (now 93) 126

Joan Sutherland: 1926 – 2010, 83 129

Nicolae Herlea: 1927 – 2014, 86...131

    Magda Ianculescu: 1929 – 1995, 65..132

    Nicolai Ghiaurov: 1929 – 2004, 74..133

    Dan Iordăchescu: 1930 – 2015, 85..133

    Anna Moffo: 1932 – 2006, 73...134

    Marilyn Horne: born 1934 (now 85) 135

    Mirella Freni: born 1935 (now 84) 135

Luciano Pavarotti: 1935 – 2007, 71 138

Plácido Domingo: born 1941 (now 78) 143

    Kiri Te Kanawa: born 1944 (now 75) 143

    René Pape: born 1964 (now 55) 145

Anna Netrebko: born 1971 (now 47) 147

    Yonghoon Lee: born 1973 (now 46)..148

    Luca Pisaroni: born 1975 (now 44) 148

    Elīna Garanča: born 1976 (now 42)...149

    Yukiko Aragaki: born 1979 (now 40) 150

Bibliography..154

Beginning of European music: 321 – 1583

321 - Roman Emperor Constantine the Great, 49, (27 Feb 272, Naissus, Dacia Ripensis (Niš, Serbia) – 22 May 337, aged 65.2, Emperor for 30.8 years: 25 July 306 (age 34.4) – 22 May 337, had 6 children) makes the day of the Sun God Sol Invictus (Sunday) a holy day, and a day of rest for Christians.

325 – 4 July - Roman Emperor Constantine the Great, 53.3, declared Christianity the official religion of the Roman Empire. The spread of Christianity in the western world encouraged the development of European music.

600 - Pope Gregory I the Great, 60, (c. 540 – 12 March 604, aged 64, Pope for 13.5 years: 3 Sep 590 (age 50) – 12 March 604, his tomb is in St. Peter's Cathedral in Vatican) codifies and collects the chant, which was used in Roman Catholic services, and in 873 was named the Gregorian chant in his honor.

circa **850** - Western music began to move from monophony to polyphony, with the vocal parts in church music moving in parallel intervals.

Guido d'Arezzo: 991 – 1033, 42

circa **1030** - **Guido d'Arezzo**, 39, (991, Arezzo, Italy - 1033, aged 42, Italian monk and music theorist, the inventor of modern musical notation that replaced neumatic notation; his book Micrologus (1025, at age 34) was the second most widely distributed treatise on music in the Middle Ages), and developed a system for learning music by ear. Voice students often use the system, called solfeggio (or solfège: *do, re, mi, fa, sol, la, si*), to memorize their vocal exercises. In the 19th century, solfeggio developed into the tonic sol-fa system used today.

circa **1180** - Troubadours appear in Germany, and call themselves *minnesingers*, "singers about love."

1430 - The Renaissance began, and this rebirth favors the virtues of Greek and Roman Classic styles, moves from polyphony to one harmonized melody, and there is an increased importance and popularity of secular music

Giovanni Pierluigi da Palestrina: 1525 - 1594, 69

1525 - **Giovanni Pierluigi da Palestrina** was born (1525 – 2 Feb 1594, aged 69, Italian Renaissance composer of sacred music, and the best-known 16th-century representative of the Roman School of musical composition. He had a lasting influence on the development of church music, and his work has often been seen as the culmination of Renaissance polyphony). He wrote the famous *Pope Marcellus Mass*.

Jacopo Peri: 1561 - 1633, 71

1561 – 20 August - **Jacopo Peri** was born (20 August 1561 – 12 August 1633, aged 71.9 (8 days before 72, his gravestone is in Chiesa Santa Maria Novella)), also known as Il Zazzerino, was an Italian composer, the inventor of opera, and the first opera singer. Jacopo Peri's *Dafne*, the first Italian opera, was produced in 1598 (age 37) and he first opera to have survived to the present day, *Euridice*, first performed on 6 October 1600 (age 39.1) at the Palazzo Pitti.

Claudio Monteverdi: 1567 - 1643, 76

1567 – 15 May - **Claudio Monteverdi** was born (15 May 1567 – 29 November 1643, aged 76.5 (his tomb is in the church of Santa Maria Gloriosa dei Frari), composer, gambist, singer, and Catholic priest). He wrote 9 books of Madrigali (1587-1643, the ninth book was published posthumously in 1651), 18 operas, but only L'Orfeo, Favola in Musica (1609), Il ritorno d'Ulisse in patria (1640), L'incoronazione di Poppea (1642), and the famous aria, Lamento, from his second opera L'Arianna (1608, sang by Virginia Ramponi-Andreini), have survived, and sacred music (Vespro della Beata Vergine (1610), Messa in illo tempore (1610), Mass of Thanksgiving (1631), Messa a 4 da Cappela (1641), and others). Monteverdi developed two styles of composition – the heritage of Renaissance polyphony and the new basso continuo technique of the Baroque. He wrote one of the earliest operas, *L'Orfeo* that is the earliest surviving opera still regularly performed.

Italy, Rome (753 BC), from Via Luisa di Savoia the north side of Porta del Popolo (1475, built on Porta Flaminia in the Aurelian Walls (275)), coat of arms of Pope Pius IV (1499-1565, on wall center up), heraldic symbols of Pope Alexander VII (1599-1667, on top center) by Gian Lorenzo Bernini (1598-1680).

Virginia Ramponi-Andreini: 1583 – 1630, 47

1583 – **Virginia Ramponi-Andreini**, also known by her stage name "**La Florinda**" was born (1583 – c.1630, aged 47). She was a celebrated Italian actress and singer, and was known for her performances in commedia dell'arte plays, many of them written for her by her 7 years older husband **Giambattista Andreini** (9 February 1576 – 7 June 1654, aged 78.3, Italian actor and the most important Italian playwright of the 17th century; married Virginia in 1601, he 25, she 18), and for having created the title role in Claudio Monteverdi's (16 years older than her) lost opera L'Arianna, in 1608, age 25, Monteverdi 41.

Caterina Martinelli: 1589 – 1608, 19

1589 – **Caterina Martinelli** was born in Rome (c. 1589 – 9 March 1608, of small pox, aged 19). She was an Italian opera singer, who was employed by Duke Vincenzo I of Mantua, 27 years older than her (21 September 1562 – 9 February 1612, aged 49.4) for 5 years, from 1603 (age 14) until her death in 1608. The title role in Claudio Monteverdi's (22 years older than her) opera *L'Arianna* was written for Martinelli, but she died prior to its premier.

Odoardo Ceccarelli: 1600 – 1668, 68

Circa 1600 - **Odoardo Ceccarelli** was born (c. 1600 – 7 March 1668, aged 68). He was an Italian singer, composer, and writer, prominent in the Sistine Chapel Choir, and the Barberini court. Ceccarelli was both a tenor and a bass, and he created roles in several operas, including Fileno in Michelangelo Rossi's "Erminia sul Giordano", and Orlando in Luigi Rossi's "Il palazzo incantato".

Anna Renzi: 1620 – 1661, 41

1620 - **Anna Renzi** was born in Rome (c. 1620 – after 1661, aged circa 41). She was an Italian soprano renowned for her acting ability as well as her voice, who has been described as the first diva in the history of opera. Anna Renzi made her debut in 1640 (age 20) at the Palazzo Pallavicini-Rospigliosi of the French ambassador, in the presence of Cardinal de Richelieu, 55, (9 September 1585 – 4 December 1642, aged 57.2, powerful French clergyman, nobleman, and statesman), as Lucinda in Il favorito del principe (music lost) by Ottaviano Castelli and the young composer Filiberto Laurenzi, who continued to function as her teacher and accompanist in later years. She was the most celebrated and highest-paid singer of the age, and Christina, 6 years younger than Anna, (18 Dec 1626 – 19 April 1689, aged 62.3 in Rome, in the extensive papal crypt at the Vatican), Queen of Sweden (6 Nov 1632 (age 5.9) – 6 June 1654 (age 27.5), for 21.6 years), was greatly pleased with Renzi's performances.

1631 - Professional female singers appear for the first time on the English stage in the production of *Chloridia*, a court masque produced by Ben Jonson and Inigo Jones.

1639 - The first comic opera, *Chi Soffre Speri* by Virgilio Mazzocchi and Marco Marazzoli, premieres in Rome.

Margarita Salicola: 1659 – 1706, 47

1659 - **Margarita Salicola** (circa 1659 – 1706, aged 47) was a famous opera singer of her time. She floruit in 1682, age 23, and was especially praised for her appearance in the title role of Carlo Pallavicino's "Penelope la casta" (The Chaste Penelope) in the winter of 1685 (age 26).

Demoiselle Conradi: 1660 – 1720, 60

1660 -**Demoiselle Conradi** (circa 1660 – 1720, aged 60), was a German opera singer. She was one of the first professional female opera singers in Germany. She was famous in her time. She was engaged at the Hamburg opera in 1690–1709, and also performed in Brunswick and Berlin.

1666 - The first signed **Stradivarius** violins emerge from Antonio Stradivari's workshop in Cremona, Italy.

1675 - Matthew Locke composes *Psyche*, the first surviving English opera.

1678 – 4 March – **Antonio Lucio Vivaldi** was born in Venezia (Venice, situated on 120 islands formed by 177 canals in the lagoon between the mouths of the Po and Piave rivers, at the northwestern extremity of the Adriatic Sea - became known as the "Queen of the Adriatic" reflecting its historic role as a naval power and commercial center), then the capital of the Republic of Venice (the strongest European power in the Mediterranean region; Venice acquired neighboring territories, and by the late 15th century, the city-state was the leading maritime power in the Christian world). He was baptized immediately after his birth, at his mother home, by the midwife, maybe because of his poor health, or because of an earthquake that shook the city that day.
Tomaso Albinoni was 7 years old (8 June 1671, in Venezia – 17 January 1751, aged 79.5), and he was an older contemporaneous Italian Baroque composer with Vivaldi.
Antonio Stradivari was 34 years old (1644 – 1737, aged 93), already famous in Cremona (60 km west of Virgilio (birthpace of the great Latin poet Vergilius, 15 Oct 70 BC – 21 Sep 19 BC, aged 50.9), 75 km southeast of Milano), north of river Po, in Lombardia, where Stradivari crafted for 81 years (from the age of 12 to 93) the best over 700 violins, cellos, guitars and harps, cold Stradivarius. The first violin was ordered by a descendent of Lorenzo de' Medici (1 Jan 1449 – 8 April 1492, aged 43.2) in 1555, in a letter to **Andrea Amati**, 50, (c 1505 – c. 1578, aged c. 73), who was the first from the Amati family of luthiers, followed by Antonio

and brother Girolamo, Niccolo, and **Girolamo** (Hieronymus II, 26 Feb 1649 - 21 Feb 1740, aged 5 days before 91).

Italy, Venezia - Piazza San Marco with Palazzo Ducale (right), Libreria Sansoviniana (next to Palazzo Ducale), Basilica di San Marco (back), Giardini Reali and Il Campanile (center-right), Procuratie Nuove (center to left), Capitano di Porto (left).

Francesca Margherita de l'Épine: 1680 – 1746, 66

1680 – **Margherita de l'Epine** was born (or **Francesca Margherita de l'Épine**; c. 1680 – 8 August 1746, London, aged 66). She was an Italian soprano, and was among the most popular of London's female singers, especially for the Italian operas, and for the operas of George Frideric Handel, 5 years younger than her (5 March 1685 – 14 April 1759, aged 74.1, burial place Westminster Abbey, London). She was close friend of the composer **Johann Pepusch**, 13 years older than her (1667 – 20 July 1752, aged 85), also known as John Christopher Pepusch and Dr. Pepusch, German-born composer who spent most of his working life in England)., whom it seems she married around 1718, at age 38, his age 51.

1681 – 24 March – Vivaldi was 3 years old when **Georg Philipp Telemann** was born (24 March 1681 – 25 June 1767, aged 86 years 3 months and 1 day, German Baroque composer and multi-instrumentalist)

1685 – 5 March - **George Frideric Handel** was born in Halle-upon-Saale (5 March 1685 – 14 April 1759, aged 74.1, burial place Westminster Abbey, London).

London - The west façade and entrance of Westminster Abbey (960, 1517, Collegiate Church of St Peter at Westminster, Anglican abbey with daily services and coronations since 1066, tower height 69 m).

31 March – **Johann Sebastian Bach** was born in Eisenach (31 March 1685 – 28 July 1750, aged 65 years, 3 months and 28 days, in Leipzig). The Bach family already counted several composers when Johann Sebastian was born as the last of the 8 children of a city musician in Eisenach, in the duchy of Saxe-Eisenach, 650 km northwest of Venezia, and 275 km southwest of

Berlin. His father, Johann Ambrosius Bach, 40, (22 Feb 1645 – 2 March 1695, aged 50), was the director of the town musicians, and all of his uncles were professional musicians. His father probably taught him to play the violin and harpsichord, and his brother Johann Christoph Bach taught him the clavichord and exposed him to much contemporary music. JSB's mother was Maria Elisabeth Lämmerhirt, 41, (24 Feb 1644 – 1 May 1694, aged 50.2). On 1 April 1668 she married the father (he was 23, and she was 24), and they had eight children, four of whom became musicians, including Johann Sebastian.

26 October - **Domenico Scarlatti** was born in Napoli, (26 Oct 1685 – 23 July 1757, aged 71.7), son of Alessandro Scarlatti (2 May 1660 – 22 Oct 1725, aged 65.4). Handel, Bach and Domenico Scarlatti were contemporaneous: Handel was 26 days older than Bach, and Bach was 6 months and 1 day older than D. Scarlatti, but D. Scarlatti died 6 years, 11 months and 25 days after Bach, and Handel died 1 year, 8 months and 22 days after Domenico Scarlatti.

<u>**1687**</u> – 5 Dec – Antonio was 9 when **Francesco Saverio Geminiani** was born in Lucca (5 Dec 1687 – 17 Sep 1762, Dublin, Ireland, aged 74.8, an Italian violinist, composer, and music theorist; he received lessons in music from **Alessandro Scarlatti**, 27, (2 May 1660 – 22 Oct 1725, aged 65.4)).

<u>**1689**</u> – **Henry Purcell**'s *Dido and Aeneas* opened in London.

<u>**1695**</u> – 2 March – Bach was 9.9 years old when his father died, 10 months and 1 day after his mother. After becoming an orphan, Bach lived for five years, until 1700, with his eldest brother, Johann Christoph Bach, 24, (1671 – 1721, aged 50), the organist at St. Michael's Church in Ohrdruf (30 km southeast of Eisenach), Saxe-Gotha-Altenburg. There he studied, performed, and copied music, including his own brother's, despite being forbidden to do so, because scores were so valuable and private, and blank ledger paper of that type was costly. He received good teaching from his brother, who instructed him on the clavichord. J.C. Bach shown him the works of great composers of the day, including South German composers such as **Johann Pachelbel** (1653, Nuremberg, Germany – 3 March 1706, Nuremberg, aged 53, under whom Johann

Christoph had studied), and **Johann Jakob Froberger** (19 May 1616 – 7 May 1667, aged 50.9, 12 days before 51); North German composers; Frenchmen, such as **Jean-Baptiste Lully** (28 Nov 1632, Florence, Italy - 22 March 1687, aged 54.3, Italian-born French (French subject in 1661, age 29) composer, instrumentalist, and dancer, who worked in the court of King Louis XIV (5 Sep 1638 – 1 Sep 1715, aged 76.9, 4 days before 77, King for 72.3 years: 14 May 1643 (age 4.7) – 1 Sep 1715) of France), **Louis Marchand** (2 Feb 1669 – 17 Feb 1732, aged 63, French Baroque organist, harpsichordist, and composer), and **Marin Marais** (31 May 1656 – 15 August 1728, aged 72.2, French composer and viol player, who studied composition with Jean-Baptiste Lully, often conducting his operas); and the Italian clavierist **Girolamo Frescobaldi** (13 Sep 1583, Ferrara, Italy – 1 March 1643, Roma, Italia, aged 59.5, Italian musician, one of the most important composers of keyboard music). Also, during this time, he was taught theology, Latin, Greek, French, and Italian at the local gymnasium in Ohrdruf.

21 November – Antonio was 17.6 when **Henry Purcell** died, aged 36.2 (10 Sep 1659 – 21 Nov 1695, English composer).

1700 – Vivaldi was 22 when, with the patronage of the Grand Prince Ferdinando de' Medici, 37, (9 Aug 1663 in Palazzo Pitti, Firenze, Toscana – 31 Oct 1713 in the same Palazzo Pitti, aged 50.2), **Bartolomeo Cristofori**, 45, (4 May 1655 – 27 Jan 1731 (aged 75.7) hired in 1688 (age 33)), invented the piano.

Germany - 23 March 1978, Freibourg im Breisgau (1120 by Duke Berthold III of Zähringen (1085-1122), elevation 278 m, the south façade of Freiburger Münster (cathedral, 1200, 116 m, J. S. Bach (1685-1750) performed here).

1709 – 8 February - **Giuseppe Torelli** died in Bologna at 50.8 (22 April 1658, Verona – 8 Feb 1709, Italian violist, violinist, teacher, and composer of instrumental concerti, especially concerti grossi, and solo concerti, for strings and continuo, and the most prolific Baroque composer for trumpets).

1710 – 4 January - **Giovanni Battista Pergolesi** was born (4 Jan 1710 – 16 March 1736, aged 26.2, Italian composer, violinist and organist; his best-known works include his Stabat Mater and the opera *La serva padrona* (*The Maid Turned Mistress*)).

1712 – 28 June – Vivaldi was 34.2 when **Jean-Jacques Rousseau** was born in Geneva, Switzerland (28 June 1712, – 2 July 1778, Ermenonville, France, aged 65.9, 4 days before 66, Genevan philosopher, writer, and composer).

1713 – 8 January – Vivaldi was 34.8 when **Arcangelo Corelli** died at 59.9 (17 February 1653 – 8 January 1713, Italian violinist and composer of the Baroque era, older contemporaneous with Giuseppe Torelli (Corelli was born 5.2 years before Torelli, and died 3.9 years after him)).

Anna Tessieri Girò: 1710 – 1750, 40

1719 – Vivaldi, 41, in Matua, produced several operas, among them Armida, Teuzzone, and Tito Manlio (RV 738; on the score of this opera are the words: "music by Vivaldi, made in 5 days.").

Vivaldi became acquainted with an aspiring young singer **Anna Tessieri Girò** (or Giraud) (circa 1710 in Mantua – 1750, aged 40, Italian mezzo-soprano, debuted in 1723 (age 13), and she was a prima donna for 22 years, until 1748 (age 38), when she married a Count, and retired from performing), who would become his student this year (age 10), protégée (age 14), and favorite *prima donna* (age 16). Anna, 32 years younger than Vivaldi, along with her older half-sister Paolina, moved in to live with him, became part of Vivaldi's entourage, and regularly accompanied him on his many travels. There was speculation as to the nature of Vivaldi's and Girò's relationship, but no evidence exists to indicate anything beyond friendship, and professional collaboration. Vivaldi maintained that she was no more than a housekeeper and good friend, just like Anna's half-sister, Paolina, who also shared his house. In his Memoirs, written around 1790, the Italian playwright Carlo Goldoni (25 Feb 1707, Venezia, - 6 Feb 1793, Paris, aged 85.9, 19 days before 86; he worked with Vivaldi, 29 years older than him, after 1729) gave the following portrait of Vivaldi and Giraud, probably from 1729 (Vivaldi 51, Giraud 19, Goldoni 22): "This priest, an excellent violinist, has trained Miss Giraud to be a singer. She was young, born in Venice (in reality Mantua), but the daughter of a French wigmaker. She was not beautiful, though she was elegant, small in stature, with beautiful eyes, and a fascinating mouth. She had a small voice, but many languages in which to harangue." Vivaldi stayed together with her most of the time.

George Frideric Handel was born 26 days before Bach, in Halle-upon-Saale (130 km northeast of Eisenach, and 30 km south of Köthen) (5 March 1685 – 14 April 1759, aged 74.1, burial place Westminster Abbey, London). Despite being of the same age, and living less than 130 km apart, Bach and Handel never met. In 1719, Bach made the 30-km south journey from Köthen to Halle, with the intention of meeting Handel, however, Handel had left the town.

London - From the Mall, looking southwest to the Victoria Memorial (1911, center left) and to the Buckingham Palace (1703).

1723 – Vivaldi, 45, composed "Le Quattro Stagioni" ("The Four Seasons") - four violin concertos that give musical expression to the seasons of the year. Though three of the concerti are wholly original, the first, "Primavera (Spring)", borrows motifs from a Sinfonia in the first act of Vivaldi's contemporaneous opera *Il Giustino*. The inspiration for the concertos was probably the countryside around Mantua, where he was 4 years ago. They were a big novelty in musical conception: in them Vivaldi represented flowing creeks, singing birds (of different species, each specifically characterized), barking dogs, buzzing mosquitoes, crying shepherds, storms, drunken dancers, silent nights, hunting parties from both the hunters' and the prey's point of view, frozen landscapes, ice-skating children, and warming winter fires. Each concerto is associated with a sonnet, possibly by Vivaldi, describing the scenes depicted in the music.

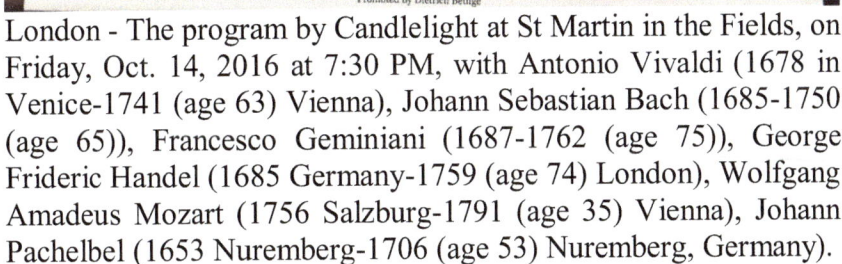

London - The program by Candlelight at St Martin in the Fields, on Friday, Oct. 14, 2016 at 7:30 PM, with Antonio Vivaldi (1678 in Venice-1741 (age 63) Vienna), Johann Sebastian Bach (1685-1750 (age 65)), Francesco Geminiani (1687-1762 (age 75)), George Frideric Handel (1685 Germany-1759 (age 74) London), Wolfgang Amadeus Mozart (1756 Salzburg-1791 (age 35) Vienna), Johann Pachelbel (1653 Nuremberg-1706 (age 53) Nuremberg, Germany).

1727 – Vivaldi, 49, composed the "Stabat Mater", based on the hymn "The Sorrows of Mary", for solo alto voice and strings. It is a masterpiece of simplicity.

31 March – Sir **Isaac Newton** died in London, aged 84.2. Resting Place – Westminster Abbey.

The upper part of the western façade and entrance of Westminster Abbey (960, 1517, Anglican abbey with daily services, and all coronations since 1066, tower height 69 m).

1730 – Vivaldi, 52, accompanied by his father (around 75 years old), and Anna Giraud (20) traveled to Vienna and Prague (550 km northeast of Venezia), where his opera *Farnace* (RV 711) was presented in the spring. In Prague (half a century later Mozart would celebrate his first operatic triumphs there), Vivaldi met a Venetian opera company, which between 1724 and 1734 staged some sixty operas in the theater of Count Franz Anton von Sporck (for whom incidentally, Bach produced his Four Shorter Masses). In the Sep 1730 – May 1731 season, two new operas by Vivaldi were premiered there, after the previous season had closed with his opera Farnace, a work the composer often used as his showpiece.

1732 – 24 Jan, in Paris, **Pierre-Augustin Caron de Beaumarchais** was born. He will be a French polymath. At various times in his life, he will be a watchmaker, inventor, playwright (Le Barbier de Séville, Le Mariage de Figaro), musician, diplomat, spy, publisher, horticulturist, arms dealer (from France to Washington), satirist, financier, and revolutionary (both French and American). He will die just 6 months and 26 days before Washington, in 1799, at 67.3.

31 March – **Joseph Haydn** was born (31 March 1732 – 31 May 1809, aged 77 years and 2 months, an Austrian composer of the Classical period. He was a friend and mentor of Mozart (27 January 1756 – 5 December 1791, aged 35 years, 10 months and 8 days), a teacher of Beethoven (17 Dec 1770 – 26 March 1827, aged 56 years, 3 months and 9 days), and the older brother of composer Michael Haydn (14 Sep 1737 – 10 August 1806, aged 68.9).

Paris - On the façade of l'Opéra de Paris (1875): a statue and the bust of Franz Joseph Haydn (1732 – 1809), prolific and important Austrian Composer. He signed his musical work in Italian: "di me giuseppe Haydn" (by me Joseph Haydn). He wrote a great number of concertos, masses, operas, piano trios, solo piano compositions, string quartets, symphonies, baritone trios, and Gott erhalte Franz den Kaiser, which was used in Das Lied der Deutschen – Germany's national anthem.

1733 – Vivaldi, 55, concentrated mainly on operas.

Bach, 48, composed a mass for the Dresden (100 km southeast of Leipzig) court (*Kyrie* and *Gloria*), which he later incorporated in his *Mass in Re (B) Minor*. He presented the manuscript to the Elector Frederick Augustus II, 37, (17 Oct 1696, Dresden – 5 Oct 1763, Dresden, aged 66.9, 12 days before 67) in an eventually successful bid to persuade the prince to give him the title of Court Composer. He later extended this work into a full mass, by adding a Credo, Sanctus', and Agnus Dei, the music for which was partly based on his own cantatas, partly newly composed.

Bach, 48, and his wife Anna, 32, had their 10th child, and Bach's 17th child, Johann August Abraham Bach (1733 – 1733, died shortly after birth).

The comic opera, *La Serva Padrona*, from **Battista Pergolesi**'s serious opera *Il Prigionier Superbo*, impresses Europe with its humorous story and enchanting music.

1736 – Vivaldi was 58 when Bach, 51, was granted the title of court composer by the Elector of Saxony and King of Poland.

16 March - **Giovanni Battista Pergolesi** died of tuberculosis at the very young age of 26 years 2 months and 12 days (4 Jan 1710 – 16 March 1736, Italian composer, violinist and organist; his best-known works include his Stabat Mater and the opera *La serva padrona* (*The Maid Turned Mistress*)).

1737 – 14 September - **Michael Haydn** was born (14 Sep 1737 – 10 August 1806, aged 68.9).

16 November - Vivaldi, 59.6, unwaveringly denied any romantic relationship with his student and preferred prima donna Anna Girò, 27, in a letter to his patron Bentivoglio.

Antonio Stradivari died at 93 (1644 – 1737).

Bach, 52, and his wife Anna, 36, had their 12th child, and Bach's 19th child, Johanna Carolina Bach (1737 – 1781, aged 44).

1738 – Vivaldi, 60, was in Amsterdam where he conducted a festive opening concert for the 100th Anniversary of the Schouwburg Theatre.

Valentin Adamberger (Adamonti): 1740 – 1804, 64

1740 – In the spring, Vivaldi, 62, resigned from the Pio Ospedale della Pietà orphanage in Venice, and moved to Vienna, invited by the Holy Roman (Austrian) Emperor Charles VI, 54.5. On his way to Vienna, Vivaldi may have stopped in Graz (300 km northeast of Venezia), to see his former student Anna Girò, 30. Probably that Vivaldi went to Vienna to stage operas, especially as he took up residence near the Kärntnertortheater.

From this year to 1748 Bach, 55, copied, transcribed, expanded and programmed music in an older polyphonic style (*stile antico*), by, among others,
- Giovanni Pierluigi da Palestrina (1525 – 2 Feb 1594, aged 69, Italian Renaissance composer of sacred music, and the best-known 16th-century representative of the Roman School of musical composition. He had a lasting influence on the development of church music, and his work has often been seen as the culmination of Renaissance polyphony) (BNB I/P/2),
- **Johann Caspar Kerll** (9 April – 13 Feb 1693, aged 65.8, German baroque composer and organist) (BWV 241),
- **Pietro Torri** (1650 in Peschiera del Garda – 6 July 1737, aged 87, Italian Baroque composer) (BWV Anh. 30),
- **Giovanni Battista Bassani** (c. 1650 in Padua – 1 Oct 1716, aged 66, Italian composer, violinist, and organist) (BWV 1081),
- **Francesco Gasparini** (19 March 1661 – 22 March 1727, aged 66, Italian Baroque composer and teacher) (*Missa Canonica*) and
- **Antonio Caldara** (1670 in Venice – 28 Dec 1736, Vienna, aged 66, Italian Baroque composer) (BWV 1082).

Bach's own style shifted in the last decade of his life, showing an increased integration of polyphonic structures and canons, and other elements of the *stile antico*.

- 21 February - **Girolamo Amati** died 5 days before 91 (Hieronymus II, 26 Feb 1649 - 21 Feb 1740, the last of the Amati family of luthiers).

1740 – 22 February - **Valentin Adamberger**, also known by his Italian name **Adamonti**, was born (22 February 1740 (or 6 July 1743) – 24 August 1804, aged 64.5). He was a German operatic tenor. His voice was admired for its pliancy, agility, and precision, and several composers of note, such as Mozart, wrote music specifically for him. He made his opera début at Munich in 1772, age 32. This was the beginning of a successful career singing leading tenor roles in opera seria at Modena, Venice, Florence, Pisa and Rome. He created roles in operas by J. C. Bach, Giuseppe Sarti, Pietro Guglielmi, Antonio Sacchini, Ferdinando Bertoni, and others. In 1781, Valentin, 41, married the Viennese actress **Maria Anna Adamberger**, 29, (23 Oct 1752 – 5 Nov 1804, aged 52; In 1786 she, 34, starred alongside her husband, 46, as Madame Vogelsang in the original production of Mozart's singspiel Der Schauspieldirektor); their daughter was Antonie Adamberger (31 Dec 1790 – 25 Dec 1867, aged 76.99; when she was 13.6 her father died, at 13.8 her mother died; she was raised, after the death of her parents, by the poet Heinrich Joseph von Collin), later a popular actress. Valentin was liked by the public in Italy, Germany, and England, and was a particularly popular singer in Vienna. Mozart (16 years younger than Adamberger) wrote the part of Belmonte in Die Entführung aus dem Serail (1782) for him. Mozart also composed the role of Vogelsang in Der Schauspieldirektor (1786) for Adamberger, as well as several concert arias (K.420 and K.431), and the cantata Die Maurerfreude (K.471).

- 9 May - **Giovanni Paisiello (or Paesiello)** was born (9 May 1740 – 5 June 1816, aged 76). He was an Italian composer, and was the most popular opera composer of the late 1700s. His works (over 80 operas: La serva padrona, Il Barbiere di Seviglia (26 Sep 1782, Russian Imperial Court, Saint Petersburg, Russia, 33.4 years before Rossini's Il Barbiere di Seviglia), Nina, La Molinara) were praised and influenced Haydn, Mozart and Beethoven.

1741 – 28 July - **Antonio Vivaldi** died of "internal infection" (probably the asthmatic bronchitis from which he suffered all his life), in a house owned by the widow of a Viennese saddle maker, in poverty, in Vienna, Austria, at 63 years, 4 months and 24 days. In the same day Vivaldi was buried in a simple grave (like Mozart 50.4 years later), in a burial ground that was owned by the public hospital fund. His funeral took place at St. Stephen's Cathedral.

1742 – Bach, 57, and his wife Anna, 41, had their 13th and last child, and Bach's 20th and last child, Regina Susanna Bach (1742 – 1809, aged 67).

Handel's *Messiah* premiered in Dublin.

1743 – Bach was 58 when Leopold Mozart, 24, future father of Wolfgang, was appointed as fourth violinist in the musical establishment of Count Leopold Anton von Firmian, 64, (11 March 1679 – 22 Oct 1744, aged 65.6, the ruling Prince-Archbishop of Salzburg for 17 years, from 1727 to 22 Oct 1744).

Germany, Dortmund (170 km west of Göttingen), 22 March 1978, the store Besta Hungshans (left), Avis rental service (center).

Ludwig Fischer: 1745 – 1825, 79

- **1745** – Johann Ignaz **Ludwig Fischer** was born (c. 18 August 1745 – 10 July 1825, aged 79.9, commonly called Ludwig Fischer). He was a German opera singer, a notable bass of his time. While in Munich, Fischer, 34.1, married on 6 October 1779 the singer Barbara Strasser, 21, (born 1758 in Mannheim), who sang with him in Vienna, and was pensioned in 1798, at age 40. The children of this marriage all became distinguished singers: Joseph Fischer (1780 in Vienna - 1862 in Mannheim, aged 82), Josepha Fischer-Vernier (1782 - 1854 in Mannheim, aged 72), and Wilhelmine (1785 – circa 1850, aged 65). In 1779, Fischer, 34, moved to the Nationaltheater (today's Burgtheater) in Vienna. He stayed in Vienna for three years, singing about twenty different roles. In 1783 he, 38, sang with great success in Paris, in 1784 in the principal cities of Italy; starting 1785 he, 40, sang at the court of Karl Anselm, 4th Prince of Thurn and Taxis in Regensburg, and in 1789, age 44, accepted a permanent appointment at the Italian Opera in Berlin, where he worked until retiring on pension in 1815, age 70. He took some breaks from his Berlin job to sing as a guest artist in other cities: Vienna (1787, 1798), London (1794, 1798, 1812). Fischer is best remembered for the role of Osmin in Die Entführung aus dem Serail, a part made for him by Mozart (10.5 years younger than him), and which he sang in the premiere production on 16 July 1782, at age 36.9, in Vienna. In 1781, Antonio Salieri was inspired by his remarkable vocal range (Fischer could sing from a low Re (D) to a high La (A)) in composing his comic opera Der Rauchfangkehrer, writing for him the role of Herr von Bär. Fischer was a friend of Mozart. When he got into a disagreement with the Imperial theater manager, Count Rosenberg-Orsini, and decided to leave Vienna, Mozart gave him a letter of introduction to help him as he pursued his career in Paris. In 1787, when Fischer, 42, returned to Vienna for a visit, Mozart, 31, created for him the aria "Alcandro, lo confesso…Non sò, d'onde viene", K. 512, which he sang at a concert he gave in the Kärntnertortheater on 21 March.1787. Mozart added for Fisher a major aria to the first act of Die Entführung, "Solche hergelauf'ne Laffen". Fischer participated in a memorial concert for Mozart organized by his widow Constanze; he sang excerpts from La Clemenza di Tito.

Francesco Benucci: 1745 – 1824, 79

Francesco Benucci was born (ca. 1745 – 5 April 1824, Firenze, aged 79). He was an outstanding Italian bass and baritone singer of the 18th century. He sang a number of important roles in the operas of Wolfgang Amadeus Mozart (11 years younger) and other composers. In the premiere of *The Marriage of Figaro* (1786), Benucci, 41, performed the title role; Storace played Susanna. In *Don Giovanni* Vienna premiere (1788), Benucci, 43, took the role of Leporello. Mozart, 32, wrote three new numbers for the Vienna version, including the duet "*Per quelle tue manine*", K. 540b, which Benucci performed with the soprano Luisa Laschi-Mombelli. *Così fan tutte* premiered in 1790; Benucci, 45, performed the role of Guglielmo. Benucci continued in the Italian opera in Vienna until 1795 (age 50). His greatest success during this period was in *Il matrimonio segreto* by Domenico Cimarosa (1792).[19] He performed at La Scala in Milan in 1795, in operas by Giuseppe Sarti and by Angelo Tarchi. He returned to Livorno in 1797, and eventually stopped performing around 1800, at age 55.

1747 – May - Bach, 62, visited the court of King Frederick II, 35, (24 Jan 1712 – 17 August 1786, age 74.5, King at 28.3 for 46.2 years: 31 May 1740 – 17 August 1786) of Prussia at Potsdam. The king played a theme for Bach, and challenged him to improvise a fugue based on his theme. Bach obliged, playing a three-part fugue on one of Frederick's fortepianos, which was a new type of instrument at the time. Upon his return to Leipzig he composed a set of fugues and canons, and a trio sonata, based on the *Thema Regium* (theme of the king). Within a few weeks this music was published as *The Musical Offering*, dedicated to Frederick.

Bach entered Mizler's Society of Musical Sciences (1738).

Leopold Mozart, 28, future father of Wolfgang, married the future mother of Wolfgang, Anna Maria, 27, in Salzburg.

Italy, Venezia - The south end of La Piazzetta, the south part of Piazza San Marco, with gondole, and wedding pictures of a Japanese couple.

1750 – March and April – Bach, 65, becoming blind, underwent unsuccessful eye surgery.

28 July - **Johann Sebastian Bach** died in Leipzig (31 March 1685 in Eisenach – 28 July 1750, aged 65 years, 3 months and 28 days, of complications after eye surgery). He has been generally regarded as one of the greatest composers of all time, and also one of the greatest fathers, with 20 children. At Bach's death his second wife Anna was 48.8, and the remaining 9 children were: Catharina 42, Wilhelm 40, Carl 36, Gottfried 26, Elisabeth 24, Christoph 18, Christian 15, Johanna 13, and Regina 8.

Paris - On the façade of l'Opéra de Paris (1875): a statue and the bust of Johann Sebastian Bach (1685 – 1750), one of the greatest German composers and organists, who wrote the Branderburg Concertos, the Well-Tempered Clavier, over 200 cantatas, Passions, and keyboard works. Mozart, Beethoven, Chopin, Schumann and Mendelssohn were admirers of Bach. Beethoven described him as the "Urvater der Harmonie" (the original father of harmony).

Emanuel Schikaneder: 1751 – 1812, 61

1751– 17 January - **Tomaso Albinoni** died (8 June 1671, in Venezia – 17 January 1751, aged 79.5) He was an older contemporaneous Italian Baroque composer with Vivaldi and Bach (Albinoni was born 6.7 years before Vivaldi, and 13.8 years before Bach, then Albinoni died 9.5 years after Vivaldi, and almost half a year after Bach).

Bach's son Carl Philipp Emanuel, 37, saw to it that Bach's *The Art of Fugue*, although still unfinished, was published.

1 September - **Emanuel Schikaneder** was born as Johann Joseph Schickeneder (1 September 1751 – 21 September 1812, aged 61). He was a German impresario, dramatist, actor, singer, and composer, wrote the libretto of Wolfgang Amadeus Mozart's opera The Magic Flute, and was the builder of the Theater an der Wien. In the fall of 1780, the Schikaneder, 29, troupe made an extended stay in Salzburg, and at that time Schikaneder became a family friend of the Mozarts. The Mozart family at the time consisted of father Leopold (61), Nannerl (29), and Wolfgang (24). Mozart died only a few weeks after the premiere of The Magic Flute, on 5 December 1791. Schikaneder, 40, was distraught at the news and felt the loss sharply. He put on a benefit performance of The Magic Flute for Mozart's widow Constanze, 29, who at the time faced a difficult financial situation. Then his troupe mounted a concert performance of Mozart's La Clemenza di Tito in 1798, and Schikaneder maintained in the repertory six Mozart operas: Die Entführung aus dem Serail, Le nozze di Figaro, Der Schauspieldirektor, Don Giovanni, Così fan tutte, La Clemenza di Tito, and The Magic Flute. Ludwig van Beethoven, 22, had moved to Vienna in 1792 and gradually established a strong reputation as a composer and pianist. He performed in an Academie at the Theater auf der Wieden during its last years. In the spring of 1803, the first Academie at the new Theater an der Wien was devoted entirely to Beethoven's (33) works: the first and second symphonies, the third piano concerto (with Beethoven, 33, as soloist), and the oratorio Christ on the Mount of Olives. Schikaneder, 52, wanted Beethoven, 33, to compose an opera for him. After offering Beethoven an apartment to live in inside the theater building, he also offered his libretto,

Vestas Feuer. Beethoven, however, found Vestas Feuer unsuited to his needs. He did, however, set the opening scene, part of which ultimately became the duet "O namenlose Freude" from his 1804 (age 34) opera Fidelio. Beethoven continued to live in the Theater an der Wien for a while, as he switched his efforts to Fidelio.

Luísa Rosa de Aguiar Todi: 1753 – 1833, 80

1753 – 9 January - **Luísa Rosa de Aguiar Todi** was born in Setúbal, Portugal (9 Jan 1753 – 1 Oct 1833, aged 80.7). She was a popular and successful Portuguese mezzo-soprano opera singer, performing in London, Paris, Torino, Germany, Austria, Russia, Venezia, Madrid, Lisbon. In 1790, Todi, 37, started a triumphant tour through Germany, and in Bonn she performed for Beethoven, 20.

Germany, 23 March 1978, looking west to Neuenburg am Rhein (440 km southwest of Göttingen), near the border with France, Mulheim ahead (west), Breisach left (north), Schliengen right (south).

Josefína Dušková (Josepha Duschek): 1754 – 1824, 70

1754 – 6 March - **Josefína Dušková** (or **Josepha Duschek**) was born (6 March 1754 in Prague – 1824, aged 70). She was an outstanding Czech soprano, and was a friend of Wolfgang Amadeus Mozart (2 years younger than her), who wrote a few works for her to sing. In her youth Josepha studied music with František Xaver Dušek (8 December 1731 – 12 February 1799, aged 67.2), Czech composer and one of the most important harpsichordists and pianists of his time), whom she married on 21 October 1776 (she 22.6, he 44.8). When she was around 20 years old, Josepha had been the lover of the art patron Count Christian Philipp Clam-Gallas, 6 years older than her, (1748 – 1808, aged 60), and it was said that she continued to profit long afterwards from the relationship, as the Count provided her with an annuity of 900 Gulden, and even contributed to the purchase of the Villa Bertramka. Duschek, 23, met Mozart, 21, in 1777, when she visited Salzburg, where her mother was from, and she had relatives. At that time Mozart composed for her the recitative and aria "Ah, lo previdi," K. 272.

Mozart, 30, accompanied her, 32, at a private concert before the Viennese court in 1786, shortly after the success of his opera The Marriage of Figaro. Later in 1787, Mozart, 31, returned to Prague in order to complete and then produce his next opera, Don Giovanni. At this time, he stayed with the Duscheks in their summer house, called the Villa Bertramka, at Smíchov near Prague. Mozart may also have stayed there while completing his opera La Clemenza di Tito in September 1791, age 35. During the 1787 visit, Mozart, 31, wrote the concert aria "Bella mia fiamma, addio," K. 528 (it is dated 3 November 1787), and the autograph bears Josepha's (33) name in Mozart's hand.

23 August - in Palace of Versailles, France, the grandson of current King of France Louis XV (44 years old), Louis-Auguste was born – almost 20 years later he will become King Louis XVI.

Adriana Ferrarese del Bene: 1755 – 1804, 49

1755 – 11 Feb -Francesco Scipione, marchese di Maffei, or Scipione Maffei died in Verona, aged 79.7 (1 June 1675, Verona – 11 Feb 1755, Italian writer and art critic, author of many articles and plays).

- **Adriana Ferrarese del Bene** (or **Adriana Gabrieli**, or **La Ferrarese**) was born (c. 1755 in Ferrara - 1804 in Venice, aged 49). She was an Italian operatic soprano, and was one of the first performers of Susanna in Mozart's *Le Nozze di Figaro,* and the first performer of Fiordiligi in *Così fan tutte*. Adriana, 27, married Luigi del Bene in 1782, and performed thereafter as Adriana Ferrarese (or Ferraresi) del Bene. Adriana Ferrarese del Bene studied in Venice, and performed in London before arriving in Vienna, where she made her reputation singing serious roles in opera buffa.

Caterina Magdalena Cavalieri: 1755 – 1801, 46

- **Caterina Magdalena Giuseppa Cavalieri** was born (11 March 1755 – 30 June 1801, aged 46.2). She was an Austrian soprano, who studied voice with composer Antonio Salieri, 4.6 years older than her (18 August 1750 – 7 May 1825, aged 74.7, Italian composer, conductor, and teacher). Her stage debut was in 1775, at age 20, in Pasquale Anfossi's opera *La finta gardiniera.* This was followed by Ignaz Umlauf's Singspiel *Die Bergknappen* in 1778 and the role of Fräule Nannette in Salieri's *Der Rauchfangkehrer,* on 30 April 1781, age 26, a role specifically written for her, to display her virtuosity. Similarly, Mozart, 10.5 months younger than Caterina, wrote the role of Konstanze in his Singspiel *Die Entführung aus dem Serail* for her, which she premiered on 16 July 1782, at age 27.3. On 7 May 1788, Cavalieri, 33.1, sang the role of Donna Elvira in the Vienna premiere of Mozart's *Don Giovanni*. Other works by Mozart written for her are *Davide penitente* (1785), and the role of Mademoiselle Silberklang in *Der Schauspieldirektor* (1786). After 1790, Cavalieri, 35, gradually withdrew from the stage, and retired on 1 March 1793, at age 37.99. She was unmarried.

1756 – 27 January – **Wolfgang Amadeus Mozart** was born (27 January 1756, at 9 Getreidegasse, Salzburg (423 m elevation,

250 km east of Vienna, 270 km north of Venezia, ecclesiastic principality part of the Holy Roman Empire, now Austria) – 5 December 1791, Vienna, Austria, aged 35 years, 10 months and 8 days). He was baptized the day after his birth, at St. Rupert's Cathedral in Salzburg, as Johannes Chrysostomus Wolfgangus Theophilus Mozart, and was a prolific and influential composer of the classical era. Mozart showed prodigious ability from his earliest childhood. He was the son of a court musician for Sigismund Graf von Schrattenbach, 58, (28 February 1698 – 16 December 1771, aged 73.8) who was Prince-Archbishop of Salzburg for 18 years, from 1753 to 1771), and reputable violin teacher (he published in 1756 a violin textbook, *Versuch einer gründlichen Violinschule*, which achieved success), Leopold Mozart, 37, (1719, Augsburg, Germany – 1787, aged 68) and Anna Maria Mozart, 36, (1720 – 1778, aged 58). He was the youngest of seven children, five of whom died in infancy, remaining only him and his sister. His elder sister was Maria Anna Mozart, 5, (1751–1829, aged 78), nicknamed "Nannerl".

1757 – 23 July - **Domenico Scarlatti** died in Madrid (26 Oct 1685 – 23 July 1757, aged 71.7), son of Alessandro Scarlatti (2 May 1660 – 22 Oct 1725, aged 65.4).

Benedikt Emanuel Schack: 1758 – 1826, 68

1758 – 7 February - **Benedikt Emanuel Schack** (Czech: **Benedikt Žák**) was born (7 February 1758 – 10 December 1826, aged 68.8). He was a composer and tenor, a close friend of Mozart, and the first performer of the role of Tamino in Mozart's opera The Magic Flute (Schack was 33, Mozart 35). Schack was married to the former Elisabeth Weinhold, who was also a singer; she took the role of the Third Lady in the Magic Flute premiere. Toward the end of his life, around 1826, Schack, 68, was sent a letter by the former wife of Mozart, Constanze Mozart, 64, regarding a biography-in-progress of Mozart, which attests to his friendship with Wolfgang. However, Schack died before he was able to reply to Constanze's letter. Testimony for Schack's abilities as a singer comes from the father of Mozart, Leopold Mozart (1719, Augsburg, Germany –

1787, aged 68), who heard his debut performance with the Schikaneder troupe while it was visiting Salzburg in 1786 (Leopold was 67, Schack 28). Leopold wrote: "He sings excellently well and has a beautiful voice".

Salomea Deszner: 1759 – 1806, 47

1759 – 14 April - **George Frideric Handel** died in London (5 March 1685 – 14 April 1759, aged 74.1, burial place Westminster Abbey, London).

Wolfgang, 3, learned to play clavier, when his older sister Nannerl, 8, began keyboard lessons with their father, who also taught his children languages and academic subjects.

Salomea Deszner, née Teschner, Tesznar was born, (1759 - 20 March 1806, aged 47). She was a Polish stage actress, opera singer and theater director, active for 29 years, 1777 (age 18) - 1806.

London: From the northwest corner of the Tower of London (left), looking southwest to the Shard. From around 1350 for 300 years the coronation procession started here at the Tower, ending at Westminster Abbey (4 km west (right)).

Maria Aloysia Antonia Weber Lange: 1760 – 1839, 79

1760 – Mozart, 4, wrote his first melody.

- **Maria Aloysia Antonia Weber Lange** was born (c. 1760 – 8 June 1839, aged 79). She was a German soprano, with a strong association with the composer Wolfgang Amadeus Mozart (4 years older than her). Born in Zell im Wiesental, Aloysia Weber was one of the four daughters of the musical Weber family. Her three sisters were soprano Josepha Weber (1758–1819, aged 61), who premiered the role of the Queen of the Night in Mozart's The Magic Flute; Constanze Weber, the wife of Mozart; and Sophie Weber. Her half-first cousin was the composer Carl Maria von Weber. After not marring Mozart around 1777, on 31 October 1780, she, 20, married Joseph Lange, an actor at the Court Theatre who was also an amateur painter (he later produced a well-known portrait of Mozart). Mozart wrote 7 arias for Aloysia, and she sung Donna Anna, in Mozart's Don Giovanni at the Vienna premiere of the work, on 7 May 1788 (age 28), Constanze, in a revival production of Die Entführung aus dem Serail (1785–1788), and Sesto, in a Mozart widow's benefit performance of La Clemenza di Tito (1795, age 35).

Christine Rakhmanov: 1760 – 1827, 67

- **Christine Rakhmanov** was born (1760 – 1827, aged 67). She was a Russian stage actress and opera singer, who belonged to the first professional pioneer actresses in Russia. She was married to her colleague Sergei Rakhmanov, and was engaged at the Karl Knipper Theatre in St. Petersburg in 1779 (age 19), which automatically made her a member of the Imperial Theatres when the Karl Knipper Theatre was transferred to Imperial ownership in 1783 (age 23). She retired in 1815 (age 55). Christine Rakhmanov played the principal heroine roles at the Karl Knipper Theatre, and progressively came to earn great success in her roles as comical old women.

Michael Kelly: 1762 – 1826, 63

1762 – 17 Sep - **Francesco Saverio Geminiani** died in Dublin, Ireland, aged 74.8 (5 Dec 1687, Lucca, Italy – 17 Sep 1762, Italian violinist, composer, and music theorist).

25 December - **Michael Kelly** was born in Dublin, Ireland (25 December 1762 – 9 October 1826, aged 63.8). He was an Irish tenor, composer and theatrical manager, who made an international career (4 years in Italy, 4 years in Austria, 4 years in London). He had been a friend of Mozart (6 years older than him) and Paisiello (22 years older than him), and created roles in operas of both. He had a long affair with Anna Maria Crouch (4 months younger than him), whom he shared for a time with the Prince of Wales ((4 months older than Kelly) future King George IV, 12 Aug 1762 – 26 June 1830, aged 67.8)

Mozart, 6, teaches himself to play violin, and, with his father, 43, and his older sister Nannerl, 11, travel to Munich and Vienna, performing as prodigies at the court of Prince-elector Maximilian III Joseph, 35, (28 March 1727 – 30 Dec 1777, aged 50.7) of Bavaria in Munich, and at the Imperial Courts in Vienna and Prague.

Christoph Willibald von Glück composed his opera *Orfeo ed Euridice*.

Teresa Saporiti-Codecasa: 1763 – 1869, 106

1763 - **Teresa Saporiti** (or **Teresa Saporiti-Codecasa)** was born (1763, Milano – 17 March 1869, Milano, aged 106). She was an Italian operatic soprano, most remembered for creating the role of Donna Anna in Mozart's opera Don Giovanni, in the 1787 (Teresa was 24, Mozart 31) world premiere of Don Giovanni. She was an attractive woman, and performed in many places, including Leipzig, Dresden, Prague, Venice, Milano (La Scala), Parma, Modena, Bologna, Vienna, Moscow, and Saint Petersburg. Later she lived in Milan, where she held salon concerts in her house. At one of these concerts, in 1841 (age 78), Verdi, 28, presented the music for his opera Nabucco, which was to premiere the following year at La

Scala. Her daughter, Fulvia, circa 48, continued corresponding with Verdi for several years afterwards.

Anna Maria Crouch: 1763 – 1805, 42

- 20 April - **Anna Maria Crouch** was born (20 April 1763 – 2 October 1805, aged 42.5), often referred to as Mrs. Crouch, was a singer and stage actress in the London theatre. She was (briefly) a mistress of George, Prince of Wales (8 months older than her).

Cambridge, UK: From Clare Bridge (1640, 1969) over River Cam, looking north to the Garret Hostel Bridge (center back), Punting Cambridge (center right), Trinity Hall Garden (right), Clare Fellows Garden (left).

Anna Selina Storace (Nancy Storace): 1765 – 1817, 51

1765 – Michel Corrette (10 April 1707 – 21 Jan 1795, aged 87.8, French organist, composer, and author of musical method books) based his motet Laudate Dominum de coelis on Vivaldi's Primavera (Spring) from Le Quattro Stagioni.

Autumn – in Hague, Mozart, 9, and his sister, 14, were sick.

Beaumarchais, 33, wrote the well-known Figaro plays Le Barbier de Séville, and Le Mariage de Figaro, inspired from his travels in Spain in 1764, and first appeared in Le Sacristain.

- 27 October - **Anna (or Ann) Selina Storace**, known as **Nancy Storace** was born (27 October 1765, London – 24 August 1817, aged 51.8). She was an English operatic soprano. The role of Susanna in Mozart's Le nozze di Figaro was written for her, and first performed (1 May 1786) by her (age 21) – Mozart (30) directed the orchestra, playing his fortepiano. Anna's singing career as a child prodigy began in England by the age of 12, in 1777. This led to further study in Italy and to a successful singing career there during the late 1770s. While in Monza (or shortly before in Milan) in 1782, she (17) was recruited to form part of Emperor Joseph II's new Italian opera company in Vienna. Storace was recruited for Vienna along with the outstanding basso buffo Francesco Benucci (37). Storace as the prima donna and Benucci, who was also singing with her, were offered high salaries, over 4000 florins. Storace performed in about 20 operas during her stay in Vienna. Storace, 19, sang in Haydn's (age 52) oratorio Il ritorno di Tobia in March 1784. Haydn later visited Storace with her brother Stephen in their home and played chamber music. He also wrote a cantata "for the voice of my dear Storace", thought to be Miseri noi, H. XXIVa.

In Vienna, she befriended both Mozart (9 years older) and Joseph Haydn (33 years older).

On 29 March 1784, Anna, 18.3, was married to John Abraham Fisher, a 40-year-old composer and violinist, but the marriage went badly, and Fisher moved to Ireland. Storace, 19.2, was pregnant with a child, which was born on 30 January 1785; this daughter, Josepha Fisher, lived 5.5 months, until 17 July 1785. On 1 June 1785, Storace, 19.6, suffered a major failure of her voice during a performance. Anna left Vienna in 1787, age 21.3, and returned to London, where she continued her career.

When she was about to leave Vienna, Storace, 21.3, performed in a farewell concert on 23 February 1787. For this occasion, Mozart, 31.1, wrote the concert recitative and aria "Ch'io mi scordi di te? [...] Non temer, amato bene" for her. The work, which is headed "Recitativo con Rondò. Composto per la Sigra: storace / dal suo servo ed amico W: A: Mozart. / viena li 26 / di decbr: 786" (26 December 1786: Mozart was 30.9, Storace 21.1), is a duet for soprano and piano with orchestra which, in view of Mozart's note in his own thematic catalogue ("Scena con Rondò mit klavierSolo. für Mad:selle storace und mich."), was very likely performed by her, with Mozart himself playing the piano part, at her farewell concert.

In 1791, Joseph Haydn, 59, arrived in London on the first of his two visits there, during which he achieved wealth and fame, and for which composed his twelve London symphonies. Storace, 26, resumed her friendship and collaboration with Haydn at this time. She appeared in the first two of the Salomon concerts that featured Haydn's music. She also sang in the ninth and eleventh concerts, as well as in the benefit concert for Haydn, and in the concert that celebrated the awarding of an honorary doctorate to Haydn by the University of Oxford. She, 29, also performed in concerts with Haydn, 62, during his second visit in 1794/1795.

By 1808, Anna, 43, had retired from the stage.

Sofia Ulrika Liljegren (Sofia Uttini): 1765 - 1795, 30

- **Sofia Ulrika Liljegren**, also known as **Sofia Uttini** was born (1765 – December 6, 1795, aged 30). She was a Swedish-Finnish soprano, and the first professional opera singer from Finland, who was active in Sweden. Sofia Liljegren was born in Rantasalmi in Finland, and in 1781, age 16, she was engaged at the choir of the Royal Swedish Opera in Stockholm. In 1783, she, 18, was the replacement of Elisabeth Olin in the main part of *Iphigénie en Aulide* by Gluck, after which she was recommended to Gustav III of Sweden as a soloist. She married composer Francesco Uttini in 1788, age 23.

Luigi Bassi: 1766 – 1825, 59

1766 – Mozart, 10, was sick from smallpox.

- 5 September - **Luigi Bassi** was born in Pesaro, Italy (5 September 1766 – 13 September 1825, in Dresden, aged 59). He was an Italian operatic baritone. At the age of just twenty, he sang the role of Count Almaviva at the Prague premiere of Mozart's Le nozze di Figaro. The role of Don Giovanni was written specially for Bassi and Mozart rewrote Là ci darem la mano for him. Bassi moved to Leipzig, and there he sang Papageno in the Magic Flute in 1793, age 27, but shortly afterwards his singing ability had deteriorated.

1767 – 25 June - **Georg Philipp Telemann** died at 86 years 3 months and 1 day (24 March 1681 – 25 June 1767, German composer and multi-instrumentalist).

The Mozart family again went to Vienna in late 1767, and remained there for about one year, until December 1768.

1768 – Mozart, 12, writes in Vienna his first opera "La finta semplice", and a Mass.

1769 - 15 August: Napoleone di Buonaparte was born in Corsica.

December - After one year in Salzburg, Leopold, 50, and Wolfgang, 13, set off for Italy, leaving mother Anna Maria, 49, and sister Nannerl, 17, at home. This tour lasted from December 1769 to March 1771.

Italy, 6 April 1978, Pisa, Palazzo della Carovana (1562-1564) now for Scuola Normale Superiore (1810, by Napoleon Bonaparte (1769-1821), 460 students, 6% admission rate, best in Italy).

Jean Baptiste Édouard Louis Camille Du Puy: 1770 – 1822, 52

1770 – In Milan, Mozart, 14, wrote the opera *Mitridate, re di Ponto* (1770), which was performed with success. This led to further opera commissions.

17 December – Mozart was 14.9 when **Ludwig von Beethoven** was born (17 Dec 1770 – 26 March 1827, aged 56 years, 3 months and 9 days).

Jean Baptiste Édouard Louis Camille Du Puy was born (1770 in Corcelles-Cormondrèche, Canton of Neuchâtel, Switzerland – 3 April 1822, aged 52; at his funeral, Mozart's Requiem was performed in Sweden for the first time). He was a Swiss-born singer, composer, director, and violinist. He lived and worked in Copenhagen and Stockholm from 1793 (age 23) until his death in 1822. Du Puy was a very successful opera singer, starring as Don Giovanni in Mozart's opera, and he played Figaro in The

Marriage of Figaro by Mozart. By 1795, age 25, Du Puy was a member of the Royal Swedish Academy of Music, and became titular professor in 1814 (age 44).

Margareta Sofia Lagerqvist: 1771 – 1800, 29

1771 – August – December: Wolfgang, 15.5, returned with his father to Milano, for the composition and premiere of *Ascanio in Alba*.

- **Margareta Sofia Lagerqvist** was born (1771 – 6 June 1800, aged 29). She was a noted Swedish opera singer and stage actress, and was employed as an opera singer at the Royal Swedish Opera, and as an actor at the Royal Dramatic Theatre, in 1788 (age 17) – 1799 (age 28), and, additionally, as both an actor and a singer at the Stenborg Theatre in Stockholm in 1784 (age 13) – 1799 (age 28). She married her colleague Johan Erik Brooman in 1798, age 27, and became the foster mother of Hanna Brooman.

Anna Gottlieb: 1774 – 1856, 81

1774 – 29 April - Maria Anna Josepha Francisca Gottlieb (**Anna Gottlieb**) was born (29 April 1774 – 4 February 1856, aged 81.8). She was an Austrian soprano, who was the first Pamina in Mozart's opera Die Zauberflöte.

1778 – 18 June – Mozart's "Paris" Symphony (Number 31) was performed in Paris.
2 July - **Jean-Jacques Rousseau** (who was good friend with Friedrich Melchior, Baron von Grimm) died in Ermenonville, France, aged 65.9, 4 days before 66 (28 June 1712, Geneva, Switzerland – 2 July 1778, Genevan philosopher, writer, and composer).
3 July - Mozart's mother Anna Maria Mozart died at 58 (1720 – 1778).
Mozart, in Paris, with the help of his father, 59, from Salzburg, was offered a post as Salzburg court organist and concertmaster, with the annual salary of 450 florins ($63,000).

3 August – Teatro alla Scala was inaugurated in Milano, Italia.

Italy, 20 April 1978, Milano, in Piazza della Scala (Largo Antonio Ghiringhelli (1906-1979, left), looking northwest to the southeast façade of Teatro alla Scala (3 August 1778, capacity 2,800).

September – Mozart left Paris for Salzburg, passing by Mannheim and Munich. In Munich, he again encountered Aloysia, 18, now a very successful singer, but she was no longer interested in him.

1782 –16 July - Mozart, 26.5, had the premier of his opera *Die Entführung aus dem Serail* ("The Abduction from the Seraglio"), which had a great success.

4 August – Mozart, 26.6, married Constance Webber, 20.6, in St. Stephen's Cathedral, the day before his father's consent arrived in the mail. They had six children, of whom only two survived infancy.

Italy, Venezia - Libreria Sansoviniana (left), Il Campanile (center-left), Palazzo Ducale (right), and a Japanese couple wedding picture.

1784 – Mozart, 28, met Joseph Haydn, 52, in Vienna around 1784, and the two composers became friends. When Haydn visited Vienna, they sometimes played together in an impromptu string quartet. Mozart's six quartets dedicated to Haydn (K. 387, K. 421, K. 428, K. 458, K. 464, and K. 465) date from the period 1782 to 1785, and are judged to be a response to Haydn's Opus 33 set from 1781.

1785 –November – Mozart, 29.8 began his operatic collaboration with the librettist Lorenzo Da Ponte, 36.6, (10 March 1749 – 17 August 1838, aged 89.4, Italian, later American opera librettist, poet and Roman Catholic priest. He wrote the libretti for 28 operas by 11 composers, including three of Mozart's greatest operas, *The Marriage of Figaro, Don Giovanni,* and *Così fan tutte).*

Paris - The central part of the façade of L'Opéra de Paris (1875): composers Daniel Auber (1782–1871, left), Ludwig van Beethoven (1770–1827, second), Wolfgang Amadeus Mozart (1756–1791, center) and Gaspare Spontini (1774–1851, right).

1786 – 1 May - Mozart, 30.3, had the successful premiere of his opera, with him as conductor, "Le nozze di Figaro" ("The Marriage of Figaro") at Burgtheater in Vienna, librettist Lorenzo Da Ponte, based on the stage comedy "La folle journée, ou le Mariage de Figaro" by Pierre Beaumarchais (performed two years earlier, in 1784). Its reception in Prague later in the year was even warmer.

18 October - Mozart, 30.7, and his wife Constanze, 24.7, had their third child Johann Thomas Leopold (18 October – 15 November 1786, 27 days).

18 November - **Carl Maria von Weber** was born (18 Nov 1786 – 5 June 1826, aged 39.5, German composer, conductor, pianist, guitarist and critic). He was a paternal half-cousin of Constanze Mozart.

1787 –28 May - Mozart's (31.3) father Leopold, who helped his son all the time, died at 68.

The young Ludwig van Beethoven, 16.5, spent several weeks in Vienna, and probably studied with Mozart, but no reliable records survive to indicate whether the two composers ever met.

29 October – Mozart's (31.8) opera *Don Giovanni* premiered, with him as conductor, to acclaim at Estates Theatre in Prague.

15 November - **Christoph Willibald (Ritter von) Gluck** died at 73.3 (2 July 1714 – 15 Nov 1787, composer of Italian and French opera).

1788 – 7 May - Mozart's (32.3) opera *Don Giovanni* premiered, with him as conductor, in Vienna, with Donna Anna being played by soprano Aloysia Weber, 28, an older sister of Constanze, 26.3.

1790– 26 January - Mozart, one day before his 34th birthday, had the premiere, with him as conductor, at Burgtheater in Vienna, of his Italian opera buffa "Cosi fan Tutte", librettist Lorenzo Da Ponte.

1791– 5 January - Mozart, 34.9, composed the final piano concerto number 27 (K. 595 in Si bemol major (B♭)).

4 March – Mozart's piano concerto number 27 (K. 595 in Si bemol major (B♭)) was performed, with him, in Vienna.

He also composed the Clarinet Concerto K.622; the last in his great series of string quintets (K. 614 in Mi bemol major (E♭)); the motet Ave verum corpus K. 618; and the unfinished Requiem K. 626. Mozart no longer borrowed large sums from Puchberg, and made a start on paying off his debts.

26 July - Mozart, 35.5, and his wife Constanze, 29.5, had their sixth child Franz Xaver Wolfgang Mozart (26 July 1791 – 29 July 1844, aged 53 years and 3 days, composer, pianist, conductor, and teacher, whose musical style was heavily influenced by his father's mature style; he neither married nor had children).

6 September – Mozart had the premier, with him as conductor, at the Estates Theatre in Prague, of his Italian opera seria *La Clemenza di Tito,* Italian libretto by Caterino Mazzolà, 46.6, (18

Jan 1745 – 16 July 1806, Venezia, aged 61.5, Italian poet and librettist), after Pietro Metastasio (3 Jan 1698, Roma, Papal States – 12 April 1782, Vienna, Holy Roman Empire, aged 84.2, Italian poet and librettist, considered the most important writer of *opera seria* libretti). This opera is about the Roman emperor Titus Flavius Vespasianus (30 Dec 39 – 13 Sep 81, aged 41.7, emperor for 2.2 years, from 23 June 79 (aged 39.5) to 13 Sep 81). Mozart composed this opera during this year, on commission for the Emperor Leopold II's coronation festivities.

Italy, Roma - Arco di Tito (Arch of Titus, 82 AD, restored in 1821, left), and the church Santa Francesca Romana (975 – 1615, right).

Mozart fell ill while in Prague (250 km northwest of Vienna).

30 September – Mozart had the premier, with him as conductor, at Schikaneder's theatre, the Freihaus-Theater auf der Wieden in Vienna, of his German opera in the form of a Singspiel (singing and spoken dialog) *Die Zauberflöte* ("The Magic Flute"), German libretto by Emanuel Schikaneder, 40, (1 Sep 1751 – 21 Sep

1812, aged 61, German impresario, dramatist, actor, singer and composer; he played the role of Papageno)).

5 December at 12:55 AM in the night - **Wolfgang Amadeus Mozart** died in his home, probably because of a streptococcal infection (the official record wrote *hitziges Frieselfieber* ("severe miliary fever", referring to a rash that looks like millet seeds)), aged 35 years, 10 months and 8 days (27 January 1756 – 5 December 1791). His wife Constanze was 29.9, his older son Karl was 7.1 years old, and his younger son Franz was 4 months old.

Baron Gottfried van Swieten, 58.1, showed up at his home and made the funeral arrangements. He may have temporarily helped support the surviving Mozarts, as Constanze's correspondence in several places mentions his "generosity".

1792 – 29 February - **Gioachino Rossini** was born (29 February 1792 – 13 November 1868, aged 76.7, Italian composer who wrote 39 operas, as well as some sacred music, songs, chamber music, and piano pieces; he was a precocious composer of operas, and he made his debut at age 18).

15 March - Franz Xaver Süssmayr, 26, upon Constanze's request, completed Mozart's unfinished Requiem, and returned it to Constanze.

1793 – 2 January - Baron Gottfried van Swieten, 59.2, sponsored a performance of Mozart's *Requiem* as a benefit concert for Constanze, 31; it yielded a profit of 300 ducats, a substantial sum. He was also reported to have helped arrange for the education of Mozart's son Karl, 8.2, in Prague.

1797 – 31 January - **Franz Peter Schubert** was born (31 January 1797, Himmelpfortgrund, near Vienna [Austria] — died 19 November 1828, Vienna, aged 31.8). He was an Austrian composer from Vienna. Many musicians make Vienna their home, but Schubert is the only one to be born there.

- 29 November - **Gaetano Donizetti** was born (29 November 1797 – 8 April 1848, aged 50.4, Italian composer).

1801 – 3 November - **Vincenzo Bellini** was born (3 November 1801 – 23 September 1835, aged 33.9, Italian opera composer).

1803 - Beethoven produces his third symphony, *Eröica*.

1804 – 18 May - Napoléon Bonaparte, 34.7, becomes the Emperor of the French, until 6 April 1814.

1805 – 17 March - Napoléon Bonaparte, 35.6, becomes the King of Italy, until 11 April 1814.

1806 – 10 August - **Michael Haydn**, the younger brother of Joseph Haydn, died (14 Sep 1737 – 10 August 1806, aged 68.9).

1807 - Beethoven completes his *Symphony No. 5*, which is one of the best classical work ever written.

Maria Malibran: 1808 – 1836, 28

1808 – 24 March - **Maria Malibran** was born (24 March 1808 – 23 Sep 1836, aged 28.5). She was a Spanish mezzo-soprano, one of the most famous singers in operas by Gioachino Rossini, and Vincenzo Bellini.
- Napoléon Bonaparte, 39, Emperor of the French and King of Italy, annexed the Duchy of Parma and Piacenza from Italy to the First French Empire.

1809 – 3 February - Jakob Ludwig **Felix Mendelssohn** Bartholdy was born (3 February 1809 – 4 November 1847, aged 38.7). He, known as Felix Mendelssohn, was a German composer, pianist, organist and conductor. Mendelssohn's compositions include symphonies, concertos, piano music and chamber music. He had 5 children.
- 31 May - **Joseph Haydn** died (31 March 1732 – 31 May 1809, aged 77 years and 2 months, an Austrian composer of the Classical period. He was a contemporaneous friend and mentor of Mozart (27 January 1756 – 5 December 1791, aged 35 years, 10

months and 8 days; Haydn was born 23.9 years before Mozart, and died 17.4 years after Mozart), a teacher of Beethoven (17 Dec 1770 – 26 March 1827, aged 56 years, 3 months and 9 days), and the older brother of composer Michael Haydn (14 Sep 1737 – 10 August 1806, aged 68.9; Joseph was born 5.5 years before Michael, and died 2.7 years after him; Michael Haydn also was a contemporaneous composer of Mozart (Michael was born 18.3 years before Mozart, and died 14.6 years after him)).

USA, Boston: a view of the north-east part of Boston, from Cambridge, over Charles River Basin. Federal Reserve Bank Building (187 m, left), and other tall buildings in the financial district.

Giorgio Ronconi: 1810 – 1890, 79

1810 – 8 June - **Robert Schumann** was born (8 June 1810 – 29 July 1856, aged 46.1). He was a German composer, pianist, and influential music critic.

- 6 August - **Giorgio Ronconi** was born (6 August 1810, Milan – 8 January 1890, aged 79.4). He was an Italian operatic baritone, with good acting and stage presence. In 1842, he (32) created the title-role in Giuseppe Verdi's Nabucco at La Scala, Milan. Ronconi had been taught to sing by his father, Domenico Ronconi, who was a leading tenor. He married soprano Elguerra Giannoni on 8 October 1837, age 27.1, in Naples, Italy.

He made his operatic debut at Pavia in 1831, age 21, as Valdeburgo in Bellini's La straniera, and went on to sing at the Teatro alla Scala and elsewhere in Italy. In the 1830s and 1840s, he appeared in the first performances of seven operas by Donizetti:

In 1842, Ronconi, 32, appeared for the first time in London, at Her Majesty's Theatre, performing the part of Henry Ashton in Donizetti's Lucia di Lammermoor. Ronconi's success with audiences outside Italy was immediate, and he continued to be one of the most popular and influential operatic artists in Europe until the early 1870s, when he retired at age 63. From 1847 and until 1866, he appeared at London's Theatre Royal, Covent Garden, in the second and third of the three theatres on that site (now known as the Royal Opera House). Vienna heard him in 1843, age 33, and he sang in St Petersburg between 1850 (age 40) and 1860, and New York City from 1866 (age 56) to 1872 (age 62).

1813 – 9 October – **Giuseppe Verdi** was born at family's home, the first child of Carlo Giuseppe Verdi, 28, (1785 – 1867, aged 82, innkeeper) and Luigia Uttini Verdi, 26, (1787 – 1851, aged 64, spinner), in Le Roncole (90 km southeast of Milano, 90 km southwest of Verona, and 400 km northwest of Roma), a village 4 km southeast of Busseto, then in the Département Taro, which was a part of the First French Empire under Napoléon Bonaparte, 44.1, (15 August 1769 – 5 May 1821, aged 51.7, Emperor of the French 18 May 1804 – 6 April 1814, King of Italy 17 March 1805 – 11 April 1814, Coronation on 26 May 1805 at Milan Cathedral), after the annexation of the Duchy of Parma and Piacenza in 1808. Verdi full name was Giuseppe Fortunino Francesco Verdi. He was born to a provincial family of moderate means, and developed a musical education with the help of a local patron.

1814 – 6 April – Giuseppe was 5.9 months old when Napoléon Bonaparte, 44.6, ended his reign as the Emperor of the French.
11 April – Giuseppe was 6 months old when Napoléon Bonaparte, 44.6, ended his reign as the King of Italy.
4 May – Margherita Barezzi was born (4 May 1814 – 18 June 1840, aged 36.1, Verdi's wife 1836 – 1840; Verdi was 6 months and 25 days older than Margherita).

Giuseppina Strepponi: 1815 – 1897, 82

1815 – 8 Sep – Verdi was 1 year and 11 months when **Giuseppina Strepponi** was born (8 Sep 1815 – 14 Nov 1897, aged 82.2). She was an operatic soprano of great renown, starring in a number of Verdi's early operas, including the role of Abigaille in the world premiere of Nabucco in 1842 (at age 27). A highly gifted singer, Strepponi excelled in the bel canto repertoire and spent much of her career portraying roles in operas by Vincenzo Bellini, Gaetano Donizetti, and Gioachino Rossini, often sharing the stage with tenor Napoleone Moriani, and baritone Giorgio Ronconi. Donizetti wrote the title role of his opera Adelia specifically for Strepponi. Both her personal and professional life was complicated by overwork, by at least three known pregnancies, and by her vocal deterioration, which caused her to retire from the stage by the age of 31, in 1846, when she moved to Paris to become a singing teacher. While it is known that she had a professional relationship with Verdi from the time of his first opera, Oberto in 1839, age 24, they became a couple by 1847, age 32, when they lived together in Paris, then moved to Busetto in 1849 (34), married in 1859 (44), and remained together for 38 years, until the end of her life.
- Schubert, 18, wrote "Der Erlkönig," his first public success, and his most famous song.

1816 – Verdi's younger sister Giuseppa was born (1816 – 1833, aged 17).
Gioacchino Rossini's *The Barber of Seville*, based on Pierre Beaumarchais's play, debuted in Rome. His *Otello* opened in Naples.

1818 - Beethoven's (age 48) hearing has deteriorated so badly that he no longer can hear the piano, and must communicate with conversation books.

1821 – 5 May - Verdi was 7.6 years old when Napoléon Bonaparte died on St Helen Island (15 August 1769 – 5 May 1821, aged 51.7).
After Baistrocchi's death, Verdi, at the age of eight, with the help of his father, became the official paid organist.
Carl Maria von Weber's (age 35) *Der Freischutz* debuted in Berlin, and he becomes the master of German opera.

Leone Giraldoni: 1824 – 1897, 73

1824 – 4 July - **Leone Giraldoni** was born (4 July 1824, Paris – 19 September 1897, Moscow, aged 73.1). He was a celebrated Italian operatic baritone. He created the title roles of Gaetano Donizetti's Il duca d'Alba (1882, age 58) and Verdi's Simon Boccanegra (1857, age 33), as well as the role of Renato in Verdi's Un ballo in maschera (1859, age 35). Giraldoni studied in Florence with Luigi Ronzi and made his début as the High Priest in Pacini's Saffo (Lodi, 1847, age 23). He made his La Scala début as Il Conte di Luna in Il trovatore in 1850 (age 26), and during his long career sang throughout Europe with considerable success. His final performance was in Filippo Marchetti's Don Giovanni d'Austria at Rome's Teatro Costanzi in 1885, at age 61. After his retirement he taught voice and singing, first in Milan, and from 1891 (age 67) at the Moscow Conservatory. He was the author of two works on singing, and he was one of Verdi's favorite baritones. Giraldoni was married to the well-known soprano and violinist Carolina Ferni. Their son, Eugenio Giraldoni (1870–1924, aged 54), became a leading baritone like his father. In Rome in 1900, Eugenio, 30, created the role of Baron Scarpia in Puccini's Tosca.

Carlo Negrini: 1826 – 1865, 38

1826 – Verdi, 13, continuing until he was 18, wrote, as he 53 years later stated, many marches, little sinfonia used in church, concertos, variations for pianoforte, serenades, cantatas, church music.

By chance, when he was 13, Verdi was asked to step in as a replacement to play in what became his first public event in his home town Le Roncole; he was an immediate success, mostly playing his own music, to the surprise of many, and receiving strong local recognition.

Mendelssohn, 17, wrote the overture to *A Midsummer Night's Dream*, which debuted in Stettin in 1827.

- 26 June - **Carlo Negrini** was born (24 June 1826 in Piacenza – 14 March 1865 in Naples, aged 38.7). He was an Italian spinto tenor, and creator of Gabriele Adorno in Verdi's opera Simon Boccanegra. Negrini started singing in the La Scala chorus, soon making his début as a soloist in 1847, age 21, as Jacopo in Giuseppe Verdi's I due Foscari. From 1850 on, he, 24, sang major roles in Italy and Europe. In 1850 Negrini, 24, sang Gastone in Gerusalemme, the Italian language version of Giuseppe Verdi's Jerusalem, a French language re-make of I Lombardi alla Prima Crociata, in La Scala. In 1851 he, 25, sang Rodolfo in Verdi's Luisa Miller, Duca in Verdi's Rigoletto, and the title role of Donizetti's Poliuto, at the Teatro Riccardi in Bergamo (1851). In 1852, he, 26, appeared as Pollione in Norma and the title role of Verdi's Ernani at Covent Garden. In Bologna he sang in Balfe's La zingara and in Verdi's Luisa Miller. In Venice La fenice he sang in Errico Petrella's Marco Visconti (1854, age 28). In La Scala he created the roles of Don Rodrigo in Giovanni Pacini's Il Cid, (1852, age 26), Gabriele Adorno in Verdi's Simon Boccanegra (1857, age 31), Glauco in Errico Petrella's Jone (1858, age 32) and Cola di Rienzi, in Achille Peri's Rienzi, (1862, age 36). Negrini was a baritonal tenor. The tessitura for the role of Gabriele Adorno he created was so middle voiced, that Verdi later authorized transpositions up for the tenor **Emilio Pancani** in 1869 and **Francesco Tamagno** in 1881. Verdi appreciated Negrini's talent and stipulated in a contract Negrini's participation in an opera project for Naples. Verdi also sent his friend and student Emanuele Muzio to Venice to listen to Negrini in Appoloni's Adelchi. "Negrini is always a great artist", Muzio reported. "When Negrini is well he is a real gem".

1827 – 26 March – Verdi was 13.4 when **Ludwig von Beethoven** died (17 Dec 1770 – 26 March 1827, aged 56 years, 3 months and 9 days).

Francesco Graziani: 1828 – 1901, 73

1828 – Verdi, 15, wrote an eight-movement cantata, *I deliri di Saul*, based on a drama by Count Vittorio Alfieri (16 Jan 1749 – 8 Oct 1803, aged 54.7, Italian dramatist and poet, considered the founder of Italian tragedy). Verdi's cantata was performed in Bergamo (50 km northeast of Milano).

- 26 April - **Francesco Graziani** was born (26 April 1828 – 30 June 1901, aged 73.1). He was an Italian baritone and voice teacher. Graziani had his vocal attributes well suited to the high-lying operatic parts composed by Giuseppe Verdi, with whom he worked. His older brother, Lodovico Graziani (1820–1885, aged 65), was a dramatic tenor. He studied with Cellini, and made his debut In Italy in 1851 (age 23) at Ascoli Piceno in Donizetti's *Gemma di Vergy*. The next season, he sang in Macerata, performing Francesco in Verdi's *I masnadieri*. Graziani also appeared at the Salle Ventadour with the Théâtre-Italien from 1853 to 1861 (age 33), where he particularly excelled in the operas of Verdi, creating for Paris the role of Count di Luna in *Il trovatore,* and also singing Germont in *La Traviata*, the title role in *Rigoletto*, and Renato in *Un ballo in maschera*. In the summer of 1854, he, 26, performed with Max Maretzek's Italian opera company at Castle Garden in New York City. He appeared at the Royal Opera House, Covent Garden from 1855 to 1880 (age 52). His debut was on 26 April 1855 (27th birthday) as Carlos in Verdi's *Ernani*, followed by Count di Luna in Verdi's *Il Trovatore* on May 10, Riccardo in Bellini's *I puritani* on May 17, Alfonso in Donizetti's *La favorita* on May 24, and Iago in Rossini's *Otello* on August 7. He performed the role of Nelusco in

the 1865 (age 37) London premiere of Giacomo Meyerbeer's *L'Africaine*. Among the other roles he sang in London were the title role in *Rigoletto*, Renato in *Un ballo in maschera*, Posa in *Don Carlo*, and Amonasro in *Aida* (all by Verdi). His last performance at the house was as Germont in *La Traviata* with Adelina Patti on July 17 in the final performance of the 1880 season (age 52). At St Petersburg, on 10 November 1862, he, 34, created the role of Don Carlos in the first performance of Verdi's *La forza del destino*.
Graziani later moved to Berlin, where he became a voice teacher. Among his pupils was the American soprano Geraldine Farrar.

1829 – Verdi was 16 when Gioachino Rossini, 37, retired, being the most popular opera composer at that time.

In late 1829, Verdi had completed his studies with Provesi, who declared that he had no more to teach him. At the time, Verdi, 16, had been giving singing and piano lessons to Barezzi's daughter Margherita, 15.5.

Venice: Palazzo Giustinian (left), Piazza San Marco (center), Palazzo Ducale (center-right), from the east end of Canal Grande.

Antonio Cotogni: 1831 – 1918, 87

1831 – Verdi, 18, and Margherita, 17.5, were unofficially engaged.

1 August - **Antonio Cotogni** was born (1 August 1831 – 15 October 1918, aged 87.2). He was a great Italian baritone. Regarded internationally as being one of the greatest male opera singers of the 19th century, he was particularly admired by the composer Giuseppe Verdi. Cotogni had an important second career as a singing teacher after his retirement from the stage in 1894 (age 63). In 1852, he, 21, signed a contract for his debut at Rome's Teatro Metastasio, as Belcore in L'elisir d'amore. In the spring of 1857, he, 25.7, was signed for Lucia di Lammermoor and Gemma di Vergy at Rome's Teatro Argentina. The turning point in Cotogni's career came in late 1858, age 27, in Nice. By October 1860, Cotogni, 29, had sung in 21 theaters, and it was at this point that he reached La Scala, Milan, debuting there in the role of Giovanni Bandino in Bottesini's L'assedio di Firenze. In retirement, Cotogni became one of the most celebrated vocal teachers in history. He taught at Saint Petersburg Conservatory (where he had Sergei Diaghilev as a student) from 1894 – 1898 (age 67). In 1899 he, 68, was a professor at the Accademia di Santa Cecilia in Rome, where his assistant was Enrico Rosati, who was later to become teacher to Beniamino Gigli. In 1908, at the age of 77, with the tenor Francesco Marconi, he recorded the duet 'I mulattieri'" (by Francesco Masini). During his career, Cotogni was an especial favorite of Verdi's, who praised him for the beauty, warmth and strength of his voice, as well as for the emotional intensity which he brought to his musical interpretations. He sang most of the major Verdi baritone roles, and took part in the first Italian staging of Don Carlo, in Bologna, in 1867, age 36, under the supervision of the composer, age 54.

1832 - Schumann's, 22, career as a pianist is over, as one of his fingers becomes paralyzed.

1833 – Verdi, 20, went to Milan to continue his studies; he applied unsuccessfully to study at the Conservatory. He took private lessons in counterpoint, while attending operatic performances, as well as concerts of German music.

Barezzi made arrangements for him to become a private pupil of Vincenzo Lavigna, 57, (21 Feb 1776 – 14 Sep 1836, aged 60.5, composer), who had been *maestro concertatore* at Teatro alla Scala (1778, capacity 2,030). Lavigna encouraged Verdi to take out a subscription to La Scala, where he heard **Maria Malibran**, 25, (24 March 1808 – 23 Sep 1836, aged 28.5, Spanish mezzo-soprano, one of the most famous singers) in operas by Gioachino Rossini, 41, and Vincenzo Bellini, 32. Lavigna introduced Verdi to an amateur choral group, the *Società Filarmonica*, led by Pietro Massini.

Verdi's younger sister Giuseppa passed at 17 (1816 – 1833).

Ferdinando Provesi died (1770 – 1833, aged 63, Italian opera composer).

Ernesto Nicolini: 1834 – 1898, 63

1834 – 23 February - **Ernesto Nicolini** was born (23 February 1834, Saint Malo, France – 19 January 1898, aged 63.9). He was a French operatic tenor, born Ernest Nicolas. He studied at the Paris Conservatory and made his debut in 1857, age 23, at the Opéra-Comique in Halevy's Les mousquetaires de la reine. After further study in Italy, he made his debut at La Scala in Milan in 1859, age 25, under the name Ernesto Nicolini, as Alfredo in La Traviata, other roles there included Rodrigo in Rossini's Otello, and Elvino in Bellini's La sonnambula. On his return to France he sang at the Théâtre-Italien from 1862 until 1869, age 35. He made his debut at the Royal Opera House, Covent Garden, in London in 1866, age 32, as Edgardo in Lucia di Lammermoor.

Five years later he returned to London to sing in Faust and Robert le diable at Drury Lane, and from 1872, age 38, appeared every season at the Royal Opera House until 1884, age 50; his roles there included Pery in Il Guarany, Radames in Aida, and the title role in Lohengrin. He created the role of Celio at the premiere of Charles Lenepveu's Velléda in 1882, age 48.

During the season 1874 – 1875, he, 40, appeared in St Petersburg and Moscow, with the world-famous soprano Adelina Patti, 31, whom he would partner in almost all her appearances thereafter, accompanying her on concert tours of the major western European capitals (Vienna, Milan, Venice, Brussels, Berlin, and so on), as well on tours of the United States, and South America.

While together in Paris in 1886, he 52, she 43, singing in Faust at the Grand Opéra, the two married; Patti had divorced her first husband, the Marquis de Caux, shortly before her wedding to Nicolini. Nicolini appeared on stage for the last time at Drury Lane in 1897, age 63, as Almaviva in Il Barbiere di Siviglia. He died the following year in Pau, France.

Charles Santley: 1834 -1922, 88

1834 - 28 February – **Sir Charles Santley** was born (28 February 1834 – 22 September 1922, aged 88.6). He was an English-born opera and oratorio baritone. Santley appeared in many major opera and oratorio productions in Great Britain and North America, giving numerous recitals as well. He made his debut in Italy in 1857, age 23, after undertaking vocal studies in that country. Santley retired from opera during the 1870s, age 40. Santley also wrote books on vocal technique, and two sets of memoirs. In 1855, Santley, 21, went to Italy to study as a singer, under Gaetano Nava, who became his lifelong friend. Nava taught him buffo roles in Rossini's La Cenerentola, L'italiana in Algeri and Il Turco in Italia, and in Mercadante's operas, laying the basis of sound vocal technique as a baritone. He also taught him Italian speech. Santley studied duets from Bellini's Zaira and Rossini's Semiramide and The Siege of Corinth. He was a frequent guest at concerts and conversaziones of the Marani family. At the theatres he heard Antonio Giuglini, Scheggi, Marini and Enrico Delle Sedie, and saw Ristori in Maria Stuarda, attending La Scala, Milan, and the Carcano Theatre. He made his stage debut on 1 January 1857, age 22.8, in Pavia as Dr. Grenvill in La Traviata (later in the same run singing Germont père), and Don Silva in Ernani. Back to England, Mapleson invited Santley back for his own Italian opera company, and in the 1862 - 1863 season at Majesty's, he, 28, performed in Il Trovatore (as Di Luna), The Marriage of Figaro (as Almaviva) and Les Huguenots (as de Nevers). In November 1864 he, 30.7, went to Barcelona, for a three-month season at the Liceu. His Di Luna was warmly received, and he followed with his first Rigoletto, and La Traviata. He also played Enrico in Lucia, Obertal in Le Prophète, and Renato in Un ballo in maschera. Later he performed Carlo Quinto in Ernani for the first time, and sang at the Theatre Royal at Liverpool. The year 1867 brought the engagement of Sweden's Christine Nilsson, and Santley, 33, appeared with her in La Traviata and I Lombardi. La forza del destino was also given, along with Don Giovanni, Dinorah, Fidelio, Oberon, Medea, Der Freischütz and Les Huguenots. La Gazza Ladra was also staged in 1869 with Santley, 35, appearing with Trebelli, Bettini and Patti. In 1875 Carl Rosa invited him, 41, back to the stage for a season at the Princess's Theatre, London, in which he played in Le nozze di Figaro, Il Trovatore, and others. Santley then toured in Australia and New Zealand in 1889 - 1890, age 56, to the United States and Canada in 1891, age 57, and South Africa in 1893 (age 59) and again in 1903 (age 69). He sang last at the Birmingham festival in 1891, age 57, after thirty years of appearances there. Charles Santley made a few recordings, mostly of ballads. His earlier series was made for the Gramophone Company (His Master's Voice) in 1903 (age 69). Several years later he, 73, cut a group of ballad titles for the Columbia label.

Teresa Stolz: 1834 – 1902, 68

1834 – 2 June - **Teresa Stolz**, was born (2 June 1834 in Bohemia – 23 August 1902 in Milano, aged 68.2, Bohemian soprano, long resident in Italy, who was associated with significant premieres of the works of Giuseppe Verdi, and she was very close to him). She made her debut in Tiflis in 1857, age 23, and also appeared in Odessa, Constantinople, Nice, Granada and other places. In 1864 she, 30, went to Italy, where she was a pupil of Francesco Lamperti in Milan. She made her European debut in Turin in 1864. She appeared regularly at La Scala, Milan, between 1865 (age 31) and 1877 (age 43). She created the role of Leonora in the revised version of Verdi's *La forza del destino* in Milan on 27 February 1869 (age 34.6). She was the first to sing the title role of *Aida* in Italy (La Scala, 8 February 1872; age 37.6, also its European premiere). Verdi did not attend the world premiere in Cairo the previous December, and considered the Milan performance, in which he was heavily involved at every stage, to be its real premiere. Stolz was also the soprano soloist at the premiere of Verdi's *Requiem* on 22 May 1874 (age 39.9). She also appeared in the *Requiem* under Verdi's direction at the Royal Albert Hall in London in 1875. She reprised *Aida* under Verdi in Vienna in 1875 and in Paris in 1876 (age 41). Other roles included the title roles in Donizetti's *Lucrezia Borgia*, Bellini's *Norma*, and Verdi's *Giovanna d'Arco*; Mathilde in Rossini's *Guillaume Tell*, Alice in Meyerbeer's *Robert le diable*, Amelia in *Un ballo in maschera*, Gilda in *Rigoletto* and Desdemona in *Otello*. Her career took her to such places such as Moscow, St Petersburg, Cairo, the major Italian opera houses, as well as Vienna, Paris and London.

Verdi, 21, attended the *Società Filarmonica* frequently, and soon found himself functioning as rehearsal director (for Rossini's (42) *La Cenerentola,* premiered, with Rossini, 25, as conductor, on 25 Jan 1817 at Teatro Valle in Roma), and continuo player. It was Massini who encouraged him to write his first opera, originally titled *Rocester*, to a libretto by the journalist Antonio Piazza.

1835 – 23 September - **Vincenzo Bellini** died (3 November 1801 – 23 September 1835, aged 33.9, Italian opera composer).

1836 – 4 May - Verdi, 22.6, after Barezzi invited him 7 years ago to be his daughter Margherita's (now 22.1) music teacher, and the two soon fell deeply in love, being unofficially engaged for 5 years, now they were married.

14 September - **Vincenzo Lavigna** died (21 Feb 1776 – 14 Sep 1836, aged 60.5, Italian composer).

23 September - **Maria Malibran** died at 28.5, after falling from her horse (24 March 1808 – 23 Sep 1836, Spanish mezzo-soprano, one of the most famous singers).

Italy, Venezia, Libreria Sansoviniana (left), Il Campanile (center-left), Palazzo Ducale (right), and a Japanese couple wedding picture.

1837 – 26 March - Verdi, 23.4, and his wife Margherita, 22.9, had their first child Virginia Maria Luigia (26 March 1837 – 12 August 1838, 1 year and 4 months).

Verdi was working on his first opera, and he asked for Massini's assistance to stage his opera in Milan. The La Scala impresario, Bartolomeo Merelli, 43, (19 May 1794 – 10 April 1879, aged 84.9, Italian impresario and librettist, best known as the manager of the La Scala Milan opera house between 1829 and 1850, and for his support for the young Giuseppe Verdi), agreed to put on *Oberto, conte di San Bonifacio* (as the reworked opera was now called, with a libretto rewritten by Temistocle Solera, 22, (25 Dec 1815 – 21 April 1878, aged 62.3, Italian opera composer and librettist).

1838 – 11 July - Verdi, 24.7, and his wife Margherita, 24.2 had their second child Icilio Romano (11 July 1838 – 22 October 1839, 1 year and 3 months).

12 August - their first child Virginia Maria Luigia passed at 1 year and 4 months (26 March 1837 – 12 August 1838).

1839 – 21 March - **Modest Mussorgsky** was born (21 March 1839, Karevo, Russia – 28 March 1881, Saint Petersburg, Russia, aged 42 years and 7 days).

- 22 October – Verdi's second child Icilio Romano passed at 1 year and 3 months (11 July 1838 – 22 October 1839).

- 29 November - Verdi, 26.1, had the production by Milan's La Scala of his first opera, Oberto, which achieved a respectable 13 additional performances, then Bartolomeo Merelli, La Scala's impresario, offered Verdi a contract for three more works.

- The New York Philharmonic was established.

1841 – Verdi, 28, began to work on the music for *Nabuccodonosor*, the libretto of which had originally been rejected by the composer **Otto Nicolai**, 31, (9 June 1810 – 11 May 1849, aged 38.9, German composer, conductor, and one of the founders of the Vienna Philharmonic).

Autumn – Verdi's completed his opera *Nabuccodonosor*.

1842 – 9 March - Verdi, 28.5 had his opera *Nabuccodonosor* premiered at Teatro alla Scala in Milano, librettist Temistocle Solera, 26.7, based on biblical books, with the famous chorus "Va, pensiero, sull'ali dorate" ("Fly, thought, on golden wings"), and in the role of Abigaille was soprano **Giuseppina Strepponi**, 26.6, (8 Sep 1815 – 14 Nov 1897, aged 82.2, operatic soprano of great renown).

Italia, Milano - 30 Sep 2008, in Piazza della Scala (Largo Antonio Ghiringhelli (1906-1979, left), looking northwest to the southeast façade of Teatro alla Scala (3 August 1778, capacity 2,800).

- A monument to Mozart, 50.5 years after his death, was unveiled in his birthplace, Salzburg. Maria Anna Josepha Francisca Gottlieb (**Anna Gottlieb**), 68, (29 April 1774 – 4 February 1856, aged 81.8, Austrian soprano, who was the first Pamina in Mozart's opera Die Zauberflöte (The Magic Flute, 30 Sep 1791, Anna was 17.4, Mozart 35.6 (he died 2 months and 5 days later)), with help from friends, visited Salzburg for this unveiling of a monument to Mozart, and, at this event, she was the last singer alive in Vienna, who had known Mozart. Anna Gottlieb, who never married, died in Vienna at 81.8 and was buried on 6 February 1856 in the same cemetery as Mozart, the St. Marx cemetery in Vienna.

Adelina Patti: 1843 – 1919, 76

1843 – 10 February - **Adelina Patti** was born (10 February 1843, Madrid, Spain – 27 September 1919, Craig-y-Nos Castle, Wales, UK, aged 76.6). She was an Italian opera singer, earning huge fees at the height of her career in the music capitals of Europe and America. She first sang in public as a child in 1851, age 8, and gave her last performance before an audience in 1914, at age 71.

Giuseppe Verdi, writing in 1877 (he 64, she 34), described her as being perhaps the finest singer who had ever lived and a "stupendous artist". In her childhood, the family moved to New York City. Patti grew up in the Wakefield section of the Bronx, where her family's home is still standing. Patti learned how to sing, and gained understanding of voice technique, from her brother-in-law Maurice Strakosch, who was a musician and impresario.

Adelina Patti made her operatic debut at age 16.7, on 24 November 1859, in the title role of Donizetti's Lucia di Lammermoor at the Academy of Music, New York. In 1861, at the age of 18, she was invited to Covent Garden, for the role of Amina in Bellini's La sonnambula. She had a remarkable success at Covent Garden that season, and she bought a house in Clapham, and, using London as a base, went on to performing Amina in Paris and Vienna in subsequent years with equal success.

During an 1862 American tour, she, 19, sang John Howard Payne's Home, Sweet Home at the White House for the President of the United States, Abraham Lincoln, and his wife, Mary Lincoln. The Lincolns were mourning their son Willie, who had died of typhoid. Moved to tears, the Lincolns requested an encore of the song. Adelina Patti performed it many times as a bonus item at the end of recitals and concerts.

In 1869 - 1870 she, 26, engaged in tours through the Europe and Russia. Concerts in Moscow and Saint-Petersburg were very successful and Patti repeats her Russian trips during the all '70s. In Russia she made many friendships with the Russian aristocracy and musicians, such P. Tchaikovsky. In St. Petersburg, during seasons 1874-75s, Patti, 31, meet Ernesto Nicolini (in future her second husband) for the first time.

During her mature prime in the 1870s and '80s, Patti (30 – 40) had lyric roles such as Gilda in Rigoletto, Leonora in Il trovatore, the title part in Semiramide, Zerlina in Don Giovanni, and Violetta in La Traviata. In 1893, Patti, 50, created the title role of Gabriella in a now-forgotten opera by Emilio Pizzi, at its world premiere in Boston. Patti had commissioned Pizzi to write the opera for her.

She last sang in public on 24 October 1914, age 71, taking part in a Red Cross concert at London's Royal Albert Hall that had been organized to aid victims of World War I.

Patti cut more than 30-disc gramophone recordings of songs and operatic arias at her Welsh home in 1905 (age 62) and 1906 for the Gramophone & Typewriter Company. Patti's recorded legacy included a number of songs and arias from the following operas: Le Nozze di Figaro, Don Giovanni, Faust, Martha, Norma, Mignon and La sonnambula. Thirty-two Patti recordings were reissued on CD in 1998 by Marston Records.

– 11 February – Verdi was 29.3 when his opera I Lombardi alla prima crociata (time of the story: 1096-1097) was premiered at Teatro alla Scala in Milano, librettist Temistocle Solera.

March – Verdi, 29.4 visited Vienna (where **Gaetano Donizetti**, 45.3, was musical director), to oversee a production of *Nabucco*. The older composer recognized Verdi's talent, and wrote favorably about him.

Verdi, 29.5 travelled on to Parma (30 km southeast of Le Roncole), where the Teatro Regio di Parma was producing *Nabucco* with Strepponi, 27.4, in the cast. For Verdi the performances were a personal triumph in his native region, especially as his father, Carlo, 57, attended the first performance. Verdi remained in Parma for some weeks beyond his intended departure date. This fueled speculation that the delay was due to Verdi's interest in **Giuseppina Strepponi** (who stated that their relationship began in 1843). Strepponi was in fact known for her amorous relationships (and many illegitimate children, abandoned at orphanages), and her history was a difficult factor in their relationship, until they eventually agreed on marriage.

Nabucco was also performed 25 times at La Fenice in Venezia.

Italy, Venezia - Procuratie Nuove (right), Fermata San Marco (center-right), Giardini Reali (right), Chiesa San Fantin (in the back, near Teatro La Fenice), Capitano di Porto (center), Palazzo Giustinian (center-left), at the east entrance in the Canal Grande.

1844 – 9 March - Verdi was 30.4 when his opera Ernani was premiered at Teatro La Fenice in Venezia, librettist Francesco Maria Piave, 33.8, based on Hernani by **Victor Hugo**, 42, (26 Feb 1802 – 22 May 1885, aged 83.2, great French poet, novelist, and dramatist).

- 18 March - **Nikolai Rimsky-Korsakov** was born (18 March 1844, Tikhvin, near Novgorod, Russia — 21 June 1908, Lyubensk, Russia, aged 64.2). He was a well-known Russian composer.

April – Verdi, 30.5, took on **Emanuele Muzio**, 22.6, (24 August 1821 – 27 Nov 1890 in Paris, aged 69.2, Italian composer, conductor and vocal teacher. He was a lifelong friend, and the only student of Giuseppe Verdi), as a pupil and assistant. He had known him since about 1828, when they were 15 and 7, as another of Barezzi's protégés.

3 November – Verdi was 31 when his opera I due Foscari, based on **Lord Byron**'s (22 Jan 1788 in London – 19 April 1824, in Missolonghi, Ottoman Empire, aged 36.2, English nobleman, poet,

peer, and politician) play. The two Foscari, was premiered at Teatro Argentina in Rome, librettist Francesco Maria Piave, 34.5, (18 May 1810 – 5 March 1876, aged 65.9, Italian opera librettist, who was born in Murano in the lagoon of Venice, during the brief Napoleonic Kingdom of Italy).

Italy, Venezia - The Doge Francesco Foscari kneeling before the Winged Lion, the symbol of Venice, which holds the book quoting *"Pax Tibi Marce Evangelista Meus"* (Peace to you, Mark, my evangelist).

1845 – 12 August - Verdi was 31.9 when his opera Alzira was premiered at Teatro San Carlo in Napoli, based on **Voltaire**'s (21 Nov 1694 – 30 May 1778, aged 83.5, French writer, historian and philosopher) play *Alzire, ou les Américains.*

1846 – October - Verdi was 33 when Giuseppina Strepponi, 31, because of her vocal deterioration, had to retire from the stage, and she moved to Paris to become a singing teacher. Verdi gave her a love letter, which she treasured very much.

Paris - The north and east sides of l'Arc de Triomphe de l'Étoile, started by Napoleon in 1806, height 50 m, wide 45 m, deep 22 m.

1847 – 14 March - Verdi was 33.4 when his opera Macbeth was premiered at Teatro della Pergola in Firenze, librettists Piave and Andrea Maffei, 49, (1798 – 1885, aged 87, Italian poet, translator and librettist), based on **Shakespeare**'s (23 April 1564 – 23 April 1616, aged 52) play Macbeth.

22 July – Verdi was 33.8 when his opera I masnadieri was premiered, with him as conductor, at Her Majesty's Theatre in London, librettist Andrea Maffei, based on **Friedrich von Schiller**'s (10 Nov 1759 – 9 May 1805, aged 45.5, German poet, philosopher, physician, historian, and playwright) Die Räuber. Queen Victoria, 28.2, (24 May 1819 – 22 Jan 1901, aged 81.6) and Prince Albert, 27.9 (26 August 1819 – 14 Dec 1861, aged 42.3) attended the first performance, together with the Duke of Wellington, 78.2, (1 May 1769 – 14 Sep 1852, aged 83.3).

Verdi had met in London the nationalist leader Giuseppe Mazzini, who, in 1848, requested Verdi (who complied) to write a patriotic hymn.

27 July - For the next two years, Verdi lived together with Giuseppina in Paris.

Verdi was awarded, in Paris, the Order of Chevalier of the Legion of Honor.

Lilli Lehmann: 1848 – 1929, 80

1848 – 11 April - **Gaetano Donizetti** died (29 November 1797 – 8 April 1848, aged 50.4, Italian composer).

Verdi was 35 when his opera Nabucco was performed in New York.

25 October – Verdi was 35 when his opera *Il corsaro* from a libretto by Francesco Maria Piave, based on Lord Byron's poem *The Corsair*. The first performance was given at the Teatro Grande in Trieste.

- 24 November - **Lilli Lehmann**, was born as Elisabeth Maria Lehmann, later Elisabeth Maria Lehmann-Kalisch (24 November 1848 – 17 May 1929, aged 80.5). She was a German operatic soprano of great versatility, and also a voice teacher. After singing small parts on the stage, for example in Mozart's Magic Flute at Prague in 1866, age 18, and studies under Heinrich Laube in Leipzig, Lehmann made her proper debut in 1870, age 22, in Berlin, as a light soprano in Meyerbeer's Das Feldlager in Schlesien. She subsequently became so successful that she was appointed an Imperial Chamber Singer for life in 1876, age 28. Lehmann sang in the first Bayreuth Festival in 1876. She performed in London in 1884, age 36, and appeared at the New York Metropolitan Opera in 1885 (37) – 1899 (age 51). She appeared at London's Royal Opera House, Covent Garden, in 1899, and sang in Paris and Vienna in 1903 (age 55) and 1909 (age 61) respectively. In 1905, she, 57, sang at the Salzburg Festival, later becoming the festival's artistic director. Lehmann was also renowned as a Lieder singer. She continued to give recitals until her retirement from the concert stage in the 1920s (age 73). She performed 170 different parts in a total of 119 German, Italian and French operas. She was also a noted voice teacher. Among her pupils were the famous sopranos Geraldine Farrar, Viorica Ursuleac, Edytha Fleischer, Olive Fremstad and the mezzo-sopranos Lula Mysz-Gmeiner and Marion

Telva. In 1888, she, 40, married the tenor Paul Kalisch. Lehmann founded the International Summer Academy at the Mozarteum in Salzburg in 1916, age 68. The Lilli Lehmann Medal is awarded by the Mozarteum in her honor. Her voice can be heard on CD reissues of the recordings which she, 62, made prior to World War I.

22 Oct 2009, in Piazza Giuseppe Verdi, looking north to Teatro Lirico Giuseppe Verdi (1813-1901). with Stagione sinfonica 2009, which includes Mozart (1756-1791), Haydn (1732-1809), Paganini (1782-1840), von Weber (1786-1826), and Respighi (1879-1936).

1849 – 27 January – Verdi was 35.3 when his opera *La battaglia di Legnano* was premiered at Teatro Argentina in Roma, libretto by Salvadore Cammarano, 47.9, (19 March 1801 – 17 July 1852, aged 51.3). It was based on the play *La Bataille de Toulouse* by **Joseph Méry**, 52, (21 January 1797 – 17 June 1866, aged 69.4, French writer, journalist, novelist, poet, playwright and librettist), later the co-librettist of Verdi's *Don Carlos*.

11 May – Verdi was 35.6 when **Otto Nicolai** died (9 June 1810 – 11 May 1849, aged 38.9, German composer, conductor, and one of the founders of the Vienna Philharmonic).

July - Verdi and Strepponi left Paris because an outbreak of cholera, and went directly to Busseto, where they lived together, which created serious problems.

Verdi worked on his opera Luisa Miller.

8 December – Verdi was 36.2 when his opera Luisa Miller was premiered at Teatro San Carlo in Napoli, librettist Salvadore Cammarano, 48.7, based on the play *Kabale und Liebe* (*Intrigue and Love*) by the German dramatist **Friedrich von Schiller**.

Sofia Scalchi: 1850 – 1922, 71

1850 – Verdi was 37 when his opera Nabucco was performed in Buenos Aires.

16 November - Verdi was 37.1 when his opera Stiffelio was premiered at Teatro Grande in Trieste, Italian libretto by Francesco Maria Piave.

- 29 November - **Sofia Scalchi** was born (29 November 1850 – 22 August 1922, aged 71.7). She was an Italian operatic contralto, who could also sing in the mezzo-soprano range. Her career was international, and she appeared at leading theatres in both Europe and America. In 1866, she, 16, made her stage debut in Mantua as Ulrica in Giuseppe Verdi's *Un ballo in maschera*.

Her first major international success came at the Royal Opera House, Covent Garden, where on 5 November 1868, she, 17.9, made her London debut as Azucena in *Il trovatore*, by Verdi. She appeared with the Covent Garden company thereafter until 1890, age 40, performing most of the standard lower-pitched female operatic roles, including Urbain, Amneris and Arsace. Meanwhile, in 1882 - 1883, she, 32, toured the United States for the first time, singing on that occasion with Mapleson's company.

Scalchi, 32.9, sang in the newly constructed New York City Metropolitan Opera's first ever staged work, Charles Gounod's *Faust*, which inaugurated the theatre on 22 October 1883. She returned to Mapleson's troupe a year later, but went back to the Metropolitan in 1891, where she, 41, would spend five further seasons. She did take part in a number of important American premieres, including those of Verdi's last two masterpieces, *Otello* and *Falstaff*. She appeared, too, in the initial American productions of Amilcare Ponchielli's *La Gioconda* and Umberto Giordano's *Andrea Chénier*. Scalchi retired from the Met in 1896, age 46, and formed her own private company of singers a year later, which then undertook a final American tour. In 1875 – 1876 she, 26, wed Count Luigi Alberto Lolli, an aristocrat from Ferrara, thus becoming the Countess Lolli. After her marriage, she was often addressed privately, and billed publicly on theatrical posters or programs, as Sofia Scalchi-Lolli.

Trieste - 23 Oct 2009, inside Teatro Verdi, commemoration dedicated to Claudio Monteverdi (1567-1643, composer, gambist, singer, and Catholic priest). He wrote 9 books of Madrigali (1587-1643, the ninth book was published posthumously in 1651), 18 operas, but only L'Orfeo (1609), Il ritorno d'Ulisse in patria (1640), L'incoronazione di Poppea (1642), and the famous aria, Lamento, from his second opera L'Arianna (1608), have survived, and sacred music (Vespro della Beata Vergine (1610), Messa in illo tempore (1610), Mass of Thanksgiving (1631), Messa a 4 da Cappela(1641), and others). Monteverdi developed two styles of composition – the heritage of Renaissance polyphony and the new basso continuo technique of the Baroque. He wrote one of the earliest operas, *L'Orfeo that* is the earliest surviving opera still regularly performed.

1851 – 11 March - Verdi was 37.4 when one of his greatest masterpieces, Rigoletto, premiered at Teatro La Fenice in Venice. Based on a play by **Victor Hugo**, 49, (Le roi s'amuse), the libretto by Francesco Maria Piave had to undergo substantial revisions in order to satisfy the epoch's Austrian censorship, and the composer was on the verge of giving it all up a number of times. The opera quickly became a great success.

Italy, Rome (753 BC, one of the oldest continuously occupied cities in Europe, called Roma Aeterna (The Eternal City) and Caput Mundi (Capital of the World)), in Villa Borghese (1630), a monument (1905, by Lucien Pallez, donated by the French Government) to Victor Hugo (1802 – 1885, the greatest French writer (Hernani (1830, inspired opera Ernani (1844) by Giuseppe Verdi (1813-1901)), Notre-Dame de Paris (1831), Le roi s'amuse (1832, inspired opera Rigoletto (1851) by Giuseppe Verdi)), Les Misérables (1862), Les Contemplations, La Légendre des siècles)).

1 May - Verdi and Strepponi moved into Sant'Agata, in his house, Villa Verdi, where he lived for 49.6 years, until his death.

In May Verdi also received an offer for a new opera from Teatro La Fenice in Venezia, which will be *La Traviata*.

June - Verdi's mother **Luigia Uttini Verdi** passed (1787 – 1851, aged 64).

Verdi began work on *Il trovatore* after the death of his mother, and the fact that this opera focuses on a mother rather than a father is most probably related to her death.

December - Verdi was 38.2 when he decided to go to Paris with Strepponi, where he concluded an agreement with the Opéra to write what became *Les vêpres siciliennes*.

Japan, north-west of the Sendai Station (1887), on Ekimae Dori, the restaurant Rigoletto, named after the famous opera with the same name, by Giuseppe Verdi (1813 – 1901), who wrote 37 operas, Rigoletto being the 17th, with the premiere at Teatro La Fenice, Venezia, on 11 March 1851.

1852 – February – Verdi attended a performance of **Alexander Dumas *fils'*s**, 27.5, (27 July 1824 – 27 Nov 1895, aged 71 years and 4 months, French author and playwright, best known for *La Dame aux camélias* (*The Lady of the Camellias*), published in 1848) play, *La Dame aux camélias*; Verdi immediately began to compose music for what would later become *La Traviata*.

Milano: 30 Sep 2008, poster for Corpo di Ballo del Teatro alla Scala, the ballet La Dame aux Camélias (1848) by Alexandre Dumas, fils (1824-1895), music by Frédéric Chopin (1810-1849). Much better known: opera La Traviata (1853) by Giuseppe Verdi (1813-1901).

1853 – 19 January - Verdi was 39.2 when one of his greatest masterpieces, Il Trovatore, premiered at Teatro Appolo in Rome, Italian libretto largely written by Salvadore Cammarano, based on the play *El trovador* (1836) by **Antonio García Gutiérrez**, 39.2, 5 days older than Verdi, (4 October 1813, in Chiclana de la Frontera, Cádiz – 26 August 1884, in Madrid, aged 70.9, Spanish Romantic dramatist).)

6 March – Verdi was 39.4 when his opera La Traviata was premiered at Teatro La Fenice in Venice, set to an Italian libretto by Francesco Maria Piave. It was based on Alexandre Dumas, fils' play *La Dame aux camélias*, and became the most popular of all operas, placing first in the current Operabase list of most performed operas worldwide.

This opera was Verdi's 16th in the last 11 years.

1854 – **Franz Liszt**, 43, (22 October 1811 – 31 July 1886, aged 74.7, Hungarian composer, virtuoso pianist, conductor, music teacher, arranger and organist) conducted the first performance of his symphonic poems in Weimar. The symphonic poem is an orchestral work, often in one movement, and is usually based on a literary idea. Liszt is credited with creating the genre. His symphonic poems include *Orpheus, Les Preludes* and *Mazeppa*.

1855 – 13 June - Verdi was 41.6 when his opera Les vêpres siciliennes, commissioned by the Paris Opéra, and initially given in French, was premiered, set to a French libretto by Eugène Scribe and Charles Duveyrier from their work *Le duc d'Albe*, which was written in 1838 for Donizetti.

Hariclea Darclée: 1860 – 1939, 78

1860 – 10 June - **Hariclea Darclée** was born (née Haricli; later Hartulari; 10 June 1860, Brăila, Romania - 12 January 1939, aged 78.6). She was a celebrated Romanian operatic soprano, who had a three-decade-long career. Throughout her career she participated in several world premieres, creating the title roles in Puccini's Tosca, Mascagni's Iris, and Catalani's La Wally. Puccini considered her to have been "the most beautiful and exquisite Manon". Enciclopedia dello Spettacolo, the most comprehensive international performing arts encyclopedia, named Darclée "world's greatest singer for 25 years".
She began her studies at Conservatoire of music in Iași, making her professional appearances as a concert performer in 1884, age 24.
She continued her studies in Paris, with Jean-Baptiste Faure. She married a young officer, Iorgu Hartulari, and became known for a while as Hariclea Hartulari-Darclée, Darclée being the nom de théâtre she adopted when she made her debut at the Paris Opéra in 1888, age 28, as Marguerite in Charles Gounod's Faust. In 1889, she, 29, replaced Adelina Patti, 45, as Juliette in Gounod's Roméo et Juliette, to increasing acclaim.
In 1890, Darclée, 30, scored a great success in her La Scala debut as Chimène in Massenet's Le Cid, and was immediately engaged by all the leading Italian theatres. Highlights of her later career in Italy from 1890 on included the world-premières of the part of Odalea in Antônio Carlos Gomes' Condor at La Scala in Milan in 1891 (age 31), the title-role in Alfredo Catalani's La Wally at the same theater in 1892 (age 32), Luisa in Mascagni's I Rantzau at the Teatro della Pergola in 1892, and the title roles in Pietro Mascagni's Iris and Giacomo Puccini's Tosca, both at Teatro Costanzi in Rome in 1899 (age 39) and 1900 (age 40), respectively. Between 1893 and 1910 she (33 – 50) appeared frequently in Moscow, St Petersburg, Lisbon, Barcelona, Madrid, and Buenos Aires. She was very popular in Spain and South America, where she participated in many local premières of new operas by Puccini, Mascagni and Massenet.
Among the many roles she portrayed are Gilda in Rigoletto, Ophélie in Hamlet, Valentine in Les Huguenots, Violetta in La Traviata, Desdemona in Otello, Mimì in La boheme, Santuzza in Cavalleria Rusticana, and the title roles in Manon, Manon Lescaut, Aida, and

Carmen. The last performance of her career was as Juliette in Roméo et Juliette at the Teatro Lirico in Milan in 1918, age 58.

Darclée's son was composer Ion Hartulari Darclée (1886 – 1969, aged 83), who was known particularly as a writer of operettas. Both she and her son are interred in Bucharest's Bellu cemetery.

Hariclea Darclée sang 58 roles in 56 operas (12 in absolute première and 16 operas in important premières) by 31 composers (19 young composers with new operas interpreted in absolute première); for this reason, Hariclea Darclée occupies a special position in the history of the opera. Started in 1995, the Hariclea Darclée Festival and International Voice Competition is held every two years in Brăila, Romania. Darclée did several recordings, which can be heard today.

Australia: In Sydney (1788, 5 M people), from the Royal Botanic Gardens looking northwest to the southeast side of the harbourfront Sydney Opera House (1959-1973, 183 m by 120 m by 65 m height, total seating capacity 5738)) and the Sydney Harbour Bridge (1932, left).

Nellie Melba: 1861 – 1931, 69

1861 – 17 March - Verdi was 47.3 when The Kingdom of Italy was officially founded, with King Vittorio Emanuele II.
 - 19 May - Dame **Nellie Melba** was born as Helen Porter Mitchell (19 May 1861 – 23 February 1931, aged 69.7). She was an Australian operatic soprano, and became one of the most famous singers of the late 19th century and the early 20th century. She took the pseudonym "Melba" from Melbourne, her home town.
Melba studied singing in Melbourne, and made a modest success in performances there. After a brief and unsuccessful marriage, she moved to Europe in search of a singing career. Failing to find engagements in London in 1886, she, 25, studied in Paris and soon made a great success there and in Brussels. Returning to London she quickly established herself as the leading lyric soprano at Covent Garden from 1888, age 27. She soon achieved further success in Paris and elsewhere in Europe, and later at the Metropolitan Opera in New York, debuting there in 1893, age 32. Her repertoire was small; in her whole career she sang no more than 25 roles, and was closely identified with only ten. She was known for her performances in French and Italian opera.
She returned to Australia frequently during the 20th century, singing in opera and concerts, and had a house built for her near Melbourne. She was active in the teaching of singing at the Melbourne Conservatorium. Melba continued to sing until the last months of her life, and made a large number of "farewell" appearances. The Australian $100 note features her image. Melba made numerous gramophone (phonograph) records of her voice in England and America between 1904 (age 43) and 1926 (age 65) for the Gramophone & Typewriter Company, and the Victor Talking Machine Company. Most of these recordings, consisting of operatic arias, duets and ensemble pieces and songs, have been re-released on CD.

December - Verdi and his wife arrived in St. Petersburg (2,200 km northeast of Milano), Russia, for the premiere of *La forza del destino*, but casting problems meant that it had to be postponed for almost one year.

1862 – 71 years after Mozart's passing, Ludwig von Köchel, 62, (14 Jan 1800 – 3 June 1877, aged 77.4, Austrian musicologist, writer, composer, botanist and publisher) published the Köchel catalogue, a chronological and thematic register of the works of Mozart. This catalogue was the first on such a scale, and with such a level of scholarship behind it; it has since undergone revisions. Mozart's works are often referred to by their K-numbers (*K* for *Köchel*); for example, the "Jupiter" symphony, *Symphony No. 41* K. 551.

24 February – Verdi, 48.2, returned via Paris from Russia, and met two young Italian writers, **Arrigo Boito**, 20, (24 February 1842– 10 June 1918, aged 76.3, Italian poet, journalist, novelist, librettist and composer) and **Franco Faccio**, 21.9, (8 March 1840 in Verona – 21 July 1891 in Monza, aged 51.3, Italian composer, conductor, between 1871 and 1889 music director of the Teatro alla Scala opera house, where he became known as a conductor of Verdi's music at La Scala, then in different parts of Italy, and abroad). Verdi had been invited to write a piece of music for the 1862 International Exhibition in London, and charged Boito with writing a text, which became the *Inno delle nazioni*.

24 May – Verdi was 48.6 when his cantata *Inno delle nazioni* was performed at Her Majesty's Theatre in London, text by Arrigo Boito.

The west façade and entrance of Westminster Abbey (960, 1517, Collegiate Church of St Peter at Westminster, Anglican abbey with daily services and coronations since 1066, tower height 69 m).

22 November - Verdi was 49.1 when his opera La forza del destino, commissioned by the Imperial Theatre of Saint Petersburg for 1861, but performed now. The libretto was written by Francesco Maria Piave, based on a Spanish drama, Don Álvaro o la fuerza del sino (1835), by Ángel de Saavedra, Duke of Rivas, with a scene adapted from **Friedrich Schiller**'s Wallensteins Lager. It was first performed in the Bolshoi Kamenny Theatre of St. Petersburg, Russia. Verdi received the Order of St. Stanislaus.

1867 – 11 March - Verdi was 53.4 when his opera Don Carlos, commissioned by the Paris Opéra, and initially given in French, was premiered at Salle Le Peletier (Paris Opéra), libretto by Joseph Méry and Camille du Locle, based on the dramatic play *Don Carlos, Infant von Spanien* by Friedrich Schiller.

After seeing Don Carlos, French composer **Georges Bizet**, 28.4, (25 Oct 1838 – 3 June 1875, aged 36.7, composer of Carmen, which became, together with Verdi's La Traviata, the most popular and frequently performed works in the entire opera repertoire) commented that Verdi is changing style.

1868 – 13 November - Verdi was 55.1 when **Gioachino Rossini** passed (29 February 1792 – 13 November 1868, aged 76.7, Italian composer who wrote 39 operas, as well as some sacred music, songs, chamber music, and piano pieces; he was a precocious composer of operas, and he made his debut at age 18).

Eugenio Giraldoni: 1871 – 1924, 53

1871 – 20 May - **Eugenio Giraldoni** was born (20 May 1871, Marseille – 23 June 1924, Helsinki, 53.1). He was an Italian operatic baritone, who enjoyed a substantial international career. In 1900, he, 29, created the role of Baron Scarpia in Giacomo Puccini's *Tosca*. He was the son of another leading baritone, Leone Giraldoni, and the soprano and violinist Carolina Ferni. His mother gave him voice lessons, and he made his opera debut in Barcelona, as Escamillo in *Carmen*, in 1891, at age 20. Giraldoni consolidated his career by appearing at various operatic venues in Italy and, in 1898 (age 27), visiting South America. Then, in 1900 (age 29), he created the part of Baron Scarpia in *Tosca*, at the Teatro Costanzi in Rome. He also appeared in the first performance of Alberto Franchetti's *La figlia di Jorio* at Italy's foremost opera house, La Scala, Milan, in 1906 (age 35). He sang in Russia and Poland from 1901 until 1907 and at the Metropolitan Opera in New York City during the 1904 – 1905 (age 33) season. In 1913, he, 42, appeared at the Opéra-Comique in Paris, as Scarpia and Sharpless. He retired from the stage in Trieste in 1921, age 50, and died three years later in Finland, where he had gone to teach. His last operatic appearance had been as the Father in *Louise*. Giraldoni made a number of recordings prior to World War I, some of which have been reissued on CD.

- 24 December - Verdi, 58.1, had his opera Aida premiered at Cairo's (2,500 km southeast of Milano) Khedivial Opera House, in Egypt. Verdi did not attend the premiere in Cairo. *Aida* was commissioned by the Egyptian government for the opera house built by the Khedive Isma'il Pasha to celebrate the opening of the Suez Canal in 1869. The opera house actually opened with a production of *Rigoletto*. The prose libretto in French by Camille du Locle, based on a scenario by the Egyptologist Auguste Mariette, was transformed to Italian verse by Antonio Ghislanzoni. Verdi was offered the beautiful sum of 150,000 francs for the opera (about $2 M now).

Japan, north-west of the Sendai Station (1887), on Ekimae Dori, the restaurant Rigoletto, named after the famous opera with the same name, by Giuseppe Verdi (1813 – 1901), who wrote 37 operas, Rigoletto being the 17th, with the premiere at Teatro La Fenice, Venezia, on 11 March 1851.

1872 – 8 February - Verdi, 58.3, had his opera Aida performed at Teatro Alla Scala in Milano, where he was heavily involved at every stage. In the role of Aida was Teresa Stolz, 37.6 (2 June 1834 in Bohemia – 23 August 1902 in Milano, aged 68.2, Bohemian soprano, long resident in Italy, who was associated with significant premieres of the works of Giuseppe Verdi, and she was very close to him), who had sung in La Scala productions from 1865 onwards.

Milano - 30 Sep 2008, in Piazza della Scala (Largo Antonio Ghiringhelli (1906-1979, left), looking northwest to the southeast corner of Teatro alla Scala (right, 3 Aug. 1778), and the Opera Museum (left)

Feodor Chaliapin: 1873 – 1938, 65

1873 – 13 February - **Feodor Ivanovich Chaliapin** was born (13 February 1873, Kazan, Russia – 12 April 1938, Paris, France, aged 65.1). He was a Russian opera singer, possessing a deep and expressive bass voice, and he enjoyed an important international career at major opera houses. Chaliapin began his career in Tbilisi and at the Imperial Opera, St. Petersburg, in 1894, age 21. He was then invited to sing at the Mamontov Private Opera (1896 – 1899 (age 26)); his first role there was as Mephistopheles in Gounod's Faust. The Bolshoi Theatre in Moscow invited Chaliapin, and he appeared regularly from 1899 (age 26) until 1914 (age 41). In addition, from 1901, Chaliapin, 28, began touring in the West, making a sensational debut at La Scala that year as the devil in a production of Boito's Mefistofele, under the baton of Arturo Toscanini. At the end of his career, Toscanini observed that the Russian bass was the greatest operatic talent with whom he had ever worked. The singer's Metropolitan Opera debut in the 1907 season, age 34; he returned to the Met in 1921, age 48, and sang there with immense success for eight seasons. In 1913, Chaliapin, 40, was introduced to London and Paris by the brilliant entrepreneur Sergei Diaghilev, 41, (31 March 1872, Russia – 19 August 1929, Venice, Italy, aged 57.4). Chaliapin toured Australia in 1926, age 53. He remained outside Russia after 1921. Chaliapin initially moved to Finland, and later lived in France. Chaliapin's last stage performance took place at the Monte Carlo Opera in 1937, age 64, as Boris. He had 9 children with 2 wives. He cut a prolific number of discs for His Master's Voice, beginning in Russia with acoustical recordings made at the dawn of the 20th Century, and continuing through the early electrical (microphone) era. Some of his performances at the Royal Opera House, Covent Garden, in London were recorded live in the 1920s. His last disc, made in Tokyo in 1936, age 63, was of the famous The Song of the Volga Boatmen. He died in 1938 of leukemia, aged 65.1, in Paris, where he was interred for 46 years, until 1984, when Feodor Chaliapin's remains were exhumed and transferred from Paris to Moscow, in an elaborate ceremony; he was re-buried in the Novodevichy Cemetery in Moscow. Many of his recordings were issued in the United States by RCA Victor. His legacy of recordings is available on CDs issued by EMI, Preiser, Naxos and other commercial labels. In 2018 his complete recordings were issued on 13 CDs by Marston Records. They consist of songs as well as a range of arias from Italian, French and Russian opera.

Rome: Fontana di Trevi (1732 – 1762). Standing 26.3 m high and 49.15 m wide, it is located on Palazzo di Poli (1566).

Enrico Caruso: 1873 – 1921, 48

1873 –25 February - **Enrico Caruso** was born (25 February 1873 – 2 August 1921, aged 48.5). He was a famous Italian operatic tenor, and still is the best tenor. He sang to great acclaim at the major opera houses of Europe and the Americas, appearing in a wide variety of roles from the Italian and French repertoires. Caruso also made approximately 260 commercially released recordings from 1902 to 1920. All of these recordings remain available today on CDs, and as downloads and digital streams. Caruso was encouraged in his early musical ambitions by his mother, who died in 1888, when he was 15. To raise cash for his family, he found work as a street singer in Naples, and performed at cafes and soirees. On 15 March 1895, at the age of 22, Caruso made his professional stage debut at the Teatro Nuovo in Naples, in the opera L'Amico Francesco, by Mario Morelli. During the final few years of the 19th century, Caruso performed at a succession of theaters throughout Italy, until in 1900 he, 27.8, received a contract to sing at La Scala, on 26 December, in the part of Rodolfo in Giacomo Puccini's La bohème, with Arturo Toscanini conducting. Audiences in Monte Carlo, Warsaw and Buenos Aires also heard Caruso sing during this period and, in 1899–1900, he appeared before the tsar and the Russian aristocracy at the Mariinsky Theatre in Saint Petersburg, and the Bolshoi Theatre in Moscow, as part of a touring company of first-class Italian singers. The first major operatic role that Caruso created was Loris in Umberto Giordano's Fedora at the Teatro Lirico, Milan, on 17 November 1898, age 25.7. At that same theater, on 6 November 1902, he, 29.7, created the role of Maurizio in Francesco Cilea's Adriana Lecouvreur. Caruso took part in a grand concert at La Scala in February 1901, age 28, that Toscanini organized to mark the recent death of Giuseppe Verdi. He embarked on his last series of La Scala performances in March 1902, age 29, creating the principal tenor part in Germania by Alberto Franchetti. A month later, on 11 April, he, 29.1, was engaged by the Gramophone & Typewriter Company to make his first group of acoustic recordings in a Milan hotel room, for a fee of 100 pounds sterling. These ten discs swiftly became best-sellers. Among other things, they helped spread 29-year-old Caruso's fame throughout the

English-speaking world. The management of London's Royal Opera House, Covent Garden, signed him for a season of appearances in eight different operas ranging from Verdi's Aida to Mozart's Don Giovanni. His successful debut at Covent Garden occurred on 14 May 1902, as the Duke of Mantua in Verdi's Rigoletto. Covent Garden's highest-paid diva, the Australian soprano Nellie Melba, 40.9, partnered him as Gilda. They would sing together often during the early 1900s. In her memoirs, Melba praised Caruso's voice. In 1903, Caruso, 30, made his debut with the Metropolitan Opera in New York City. Between his London and New York engagements, he had a series of performances in Italy, Portugal and South America. Caruso's contract had been negotiated by his agent, the banker and impresario Pasquale Simonelli. Caruso's debut was in a new production of Rigoletto on 23 November 1903. This time, Marcella Sembrich sang as Gilda. A few months later, he began his lifelong association with the Victor Talking Machine Company. He made his first American records on 1 February 1904, age 30.9. Thereafter, his recording career ran in tandem with his Met career. He also continued to sing widely in Europe, appearing again at Covent Garden in 1904 – 1907 and 1913 – 1914 (age 41), and undertaking a UK tour in 1909 (age 36). Audiences in France, Belgium, Monaco, Austria, Hungary and Germany also heard him before the outbreak of World War I. Caruso created the role of Dick Johnson in the world premiere of Puccini's La fanciulla del West on 10 December 1910, age 37.8. The composer conceived the music for Johnson with Caruso's voice specifically in mind. With Caruso appeared two more of the Met's star singers, the Czech soprano Emmy Destinn and baritone Pasquale Amato. Toscanini, then the Met's principal conductor, presided in the orchestra pit. Caruso toured the South American nations of Argentina, Uruguay, and Brazil in 1917, age 44, and two years later performed in Mexico City. In 1920, he, 47, was paid the big sum of 10,000 U.S. dollars a night (~$126,000 in 2018) to sing in Havana, Cuba. On 16 September 1920, Caruso, 47.6, concluded three days of recording sessions at Victor's Trinity Church studio in Camden, New Jersey. He recorded several discs including the Domine Deus and Crucifixus from the Petite messe solennelle by Rossini.

1874 – 22 May - Verdi, 60.6, reworked his "Libera Me" section of the Rossini Requiem, and made it a part of his Requiem Mass, honoring the famous novelist and poet **Alessandro Manzoni**, who had died in 1873. The complete Requiem was first performed at the cathedral in Milan on this day, with Teresa Stolz, 39.9.

Lalla Miranda: 1874 - 1944, 70

- **Lalla Miranda** was born (1874, Melbourne, Australia – 1944, aged 70). She was an Australian coloratura soprano, who was primarily active in Belgium, France, and Great Britain. Miranda was the daughter of opera singers David Miranda and Annetta Hirst, and the older sister of opera singer Beatrice Miranda. After studies in London and Paris, she made her professional opera debut in The Hague in 1898, age 24. She then appeared in numerous operas in Amsterdam in successive years. In 1899, age 25, she was a resident artist at La Monnaie. She made several appearances at the Palais Garnier in Paris, and at theatres in the French Provences during the first two decades of the 20th century. In 1900–1901 and from 1907–1911 she was committed to the Royal Opera House on London. In 1910 she (36) was committed to both the Manhattan Opera Company and the Philadelphia Opera Company. She notably opened the 1910 season at the Manhattan Opera House in the title role of Donizetti's Lucia di Lammermoor, a role for which she was famous. In New York and Philadelphia she also sang Gilda in Rigoletto, Olympia in The Tales of Hoffmann, and the title role in Lakmé. After 1918 she (44) was primarily active with the Carl Rosa Opera Company. She retired in the early 1920s. She made only a few recordings on the Pathé Records label.

1875 – Verdi was 62 when his Requiem, with Stolz, 41.3, was performed, under Verdi's direction, at the Royal Albert Hall in London, and then in Paris and Vienna.

London - The Royal Albert Hall (1867-1871, 2004)– an Italian style concert hall on Kensington Gore, on the northern edge of South Kensington, capacity 5,272 seats, 41 m height, named after Prince Consort Albert (1819 (in Germany)-1861), husband (1840-1861) of Queen Victoria (1819-1901, Queen 1837-1901, had 9 children), Chancellor of the University of Cambridge from 1847. In July 1871, French composer Camille Saint-Saëns (1835-1921) performed *Church Scene* from the Faust, by Charles Gounod (1818-1893).

1876 – Verdi was 63 when his Requiem, with Stolz, 42.3, was performed, under Verdi's direction, in Köln, Germany.

Pyotr Tchaikovsky, 36, (7 May 1840 – 6 Nov 1893, aged 53.5, Russian composer) completed *Swan Lake*. It opened in 1877 at Moscow's Bolshoi Theatre.

Johannes Brahms, 43, (7 May 1833 – 3 April 1897, aged 63.9, German composer and pianist) completes his *First Symphony*. Twenty years in the making, the symphony would become his most popular.

1877 - Thomas Edison, 30, (11 February 1847 – 18 October 1931, age 84.6, American inventor and businessman) invented sound recording.

Camille Saint-Saëns' (age 42) (9 October 1835 – 16 December 1921, aged 86.1, French composer, organist, conductor and pianist) *Samson et Dalila* debuted in Weimar.

1878 – 21 April – Verdi was 64.5 when **Temistocle Solera** died (25 Dec 1815 – 21 April 1878, aged 62.3, Italian opera composer and librettist).

Thomas Edison, 31, patented the phonograph.

1880 – 22 March - Verdi, 66.4, had his opera Aida performed at Palais Garnier, Paris, where he was the conductor.

Tchaikovsky, 40, wrote the *1812 Overture*.

Paris - L'Opéra de Paris (or L'Académie Nationale de Musique, or l'Opéra Garnier, or Le Palais Garnier, or L'Opéra), a 1,979-seat opera house, built from 1861 to 1875, now mainly used for ballet.

<u>**1881**</u> – 24 March - Verdi was 67.4 when the second version of his opera *Simon Boccanegra* was premiered at Teatro La Scala in Milano, Italian libretto by Arrigo Boito, 39.1, (24 February 1842– 10 June 1918, aged 76.3, an Italian poet, journalist, novelist, librettist and composer), based on the play *Simón Bocanegra* (1843) by Antonio García Gutiérrez, 67.4.
The Boston Symphony Orchestra was established.
- 19 August - **George Enescu** was born (19 August 1881 – 4 May 1955, age 73.7), known in France as Georges Enesco, was a Romanian composer, violinist, pianist, conductor, and teacher. He is regarded as Romania's most important musician.

Alice Geraldine Farrar: 1882 – 1967, 85

<u>**1882**</u> – 28 February - **Alice Geraldine Farrar** was born (28 February 1882, Melrose, Massachusetts, U.S. – 11 March 1967,

Ridgefield, Connecticut, U.S., aged 85 years and 11 days). She was an American soprano opera singer and film actress. At age 5, she began studying music in Boston, and by 14 was giving recitals. Later she studied voice with the American soprano Emma Thursby in New York City, in Paris, and finally with the Italian baritone Francesco Graziani in Berlin. Farrar created a sensation at the Berlin Hofoper with her debut as Marguerite in Charles Gounod's Faust in 1901 (age 19), and remained with the company for three years, during which time she continued her studies with famed German soprano Lilli Lehmann. She appeared in the title roles of Ambroise Thomas' Mignon, and Jules Massenet's Manon, as well as Juliette in Gounod's Roméo et Juliette. After three years with the Monte Carlo Opera, she made her debut at the New York Metropolitan Opera in Romeo et Juliette, on 26 November 1906, age 24.7. She appeared in the first Met performance of Giacomo Puccini's Madama Butterfly in 1907, age 25, and remained a member of the company until her retirement in 1922 (age 40), singing 29 roles there in 672 performances. She recorded extensively for the Victor Talking Machine Company. She was one of the first performers to make a radio broadcast in a 1907 (age 25) publicity event, singing over Lee De Forest's experimental AM radio transmitter in New York City. She also appeared in silent movies, which were filmed between opera seasons. Farrar starred in more than a dozen films from 1915 (age 33) to 1920, including Cecil B. De Mille's 1915 adaptation of Georges Bizet's opera Carmen.

Farrar had a seven-year love affair (1908 (age 26) – 1915 (age 33)) with the Italian conductor Arturo Toscanini. Her ultimatum, that he leaves his wife and children and marry her, resulted in Toscanini's abrupt resignation as principal conductor of the Metropolitan Opera in 1915. Farrar was close friends with the star tenor Enrico Caruso, and there has been speculation that they too had a love affair, but no conclusive evidence of this has surfaced. It is said that Caruso coined her motto: Farrar farà ("Farrar will do it"). Farrar retired from opera in 1922 at the age of 40.

Amelita Galli-Curci: 1882 – 1963, 81

1882 –- 18 November - **Amelita Galli-Curci** was born (18 November 1882, Milano, Italia – 26 November 1963, La Jolla, California, USA, aged 81 years and 8 days). She was and still is the best coloratura soprano, and one of the most popular operatic singers, with her recordings selling in very large numbers. In Milan she studied piano at the Milan Conservatory, winning a gold medal for piano performance, and at the age of 16, in 1898, was offered a professorship. She was inspired to sing by her grandmother. Operatic composer Pietro Mascagni, 35, (7 Dec 1863 – 2 August 1945, aged 81.6) also encouraged Galli-Curci's singing ambitions. By her own choice, Galli-Curci's voice was largely self-trained. She improved her technique by listening to other sopranos, reading old singing-method books, and doing piano exercises with her voice instead of using a keyboard. Galli-Curci made her operatic debut in 1906, age 24, at Trani (seaport in southeastern Italy, on the Adriatic Sea, 330 km southeast of Roma), as Gilda in Giuseppe Verdi's Rigoletto, and she rapidly became acclaimed throughout Italy for the sweetness and agility of her voice, and her captivating musical interpretations. The soprano had toured widely in Europe, Russia and South America. In 1915, Galli-Curci, 33, sang two performances of Lucia di Lammermoor with Enrico Caruso, 42, in Buenos Aires. These were to be her only operatic appearances with the greatest tenor, though they later appeared in concert, and made a few recordings together. Galli-Curci and Caruso also acted as godparents for the son of the Sicilian tenor Giulio Crimi (10 May 1885 – 29 Oct 1939, aged 54.4).

Galli-Curci toured extensively throughout her career, including a 1924, age 42, Great Britain concert tour, where she appeared in 20 cities and a tour of Australia a year later.

Galli-Curci arrived in the United States in the autumn of 1916, age 34. Her stay in the U.S. was intended to be brief, but the acclaim she received for her historic American debut as Gilda in Rigoletto in Chicago, Illinois, on 18 November 1916 (her 34th birthday) was so wildly enthusiastic that she accepted an offer to extend her association with the Chicago Opera Association, where she appeared until the end of the 1924 season (age 42). Also, in 1916,

Galli-Curci, 34, signed a recording contract with the Victor Talking Machine Company, and recorded exclusively for the company until 1930, age 48.

On 14 November 1921, while still under contract with the Chicago Opera, Galli-Curci, 4 days before 39, made her debut at the Metropolitan Opera in New York as Violetta in La Traviata. She was one of few singers of the era who were contracted to both opera companies simultaneously. Galli-Curci remained at the Met until her retirement from opera nine years later, in 1930, age 48.

Galli-Curci built an estate in 1922, age 40, which she called "Sul Monte" in Highmount, New York. She summered for several years there until she sold the property in 1937, age 55 (Sul Monte, was listed on the National Register of Historic Places in 2010). In the nearby village of Margaretville, a theater was erected and named in her honor. She returned the favor by performing there on its opening night

Galli-Curci retired from the operatic stage in January 1930, age 47.1, to concentrate instead on concert performances. She underwent surgery in 1935, age 53, for the removal of a thyroid goiter. Great care was taken during her surgery, which was performed under local anesthesia; however, it was thought her voice suffered following the surgery, specifically, a nerve to her larynx, the external branch of the superior laryngeal nerve, was thought to have been damaged, resulting in the loss of her ability to sing high pitches. This nerve has since become known as the "nerve of Galli-Curci." In 1908, Amelita Galli, 26, wed an Italian nobleman and painter, Luigi Curci, Marchese di Simeri, attaching his surname to hers. They divorced in 1920, age 38. In 1921, Galli-Curci, 39, married Homer Samuels, her accompanist. Their marriage lasted until Samuels' death in 1956 (her age 74).

Galli-Curci was a very popular recording artist, and her exceptional voice can still be heard on original 78-rpm records and their LP and CD reissues.

- The Berlin Philharmonic was established.

1883 - The Metropolitan Opera House opened in New York.

1886 – 25 June – Aida was presented in Rio de Janeiro, Brazil, with a locally hired conductor, who was in a two-month escalating conflict with the performers, due to his rather poor command of the work, to the point that the singers went on strike, and forced the company's general manager to seek a substitute conductor. Two other conductors tried unsuccessfully to finish Aida. In desperation, the singers suggested the name of their assistant Chorus Master, who knew the whole opera from memory – **Arturo Toscanini**, 19.2, (25 March 1867 – 16 Jan 1957, aged 89.8, the greatest Italian conductor, Music Director at La Scala: 1898 – 1908 and 1921 - 1929). Although he had no conducting experience, Toscanini was eventually persuaded by the musicians to take up the baton at 9:15 PM, and led a performance of the two-and-a-half-hour opera, completely from memory. The public was taken by surprise, at first by the youth and sheer aplomb of this unknown conductor, then by his solid mastery. The result was astounding acclaim. For the rest of that season, Toscanini conducted eighteen operas, all with absolute success. Thus began his career as a conductor, at age 19.2.

1887 – 8 December - Verdi, 74.2, had the premiere at Teatro Alla Scala in Milan of his opera Otello, based on William Shakespeare's play, with a libretto written by the younger composer of Mefistofele, Arrigo Boito, 45.8. Arturo Toscanini, 20.7, participated as cellist in this world premiere of Verdi's Otello.

Italia - 23 October 2009, Trieste (177 BC part of the Roman Republic), from Passo Fausto Pecorari, in Piazza San Giovanni, looking southeast to the statue of Giuseppe Verdi (1813-1901), and buildings on Via Giacinto Gallina (left) and Via delle Torri (right).

1888 – Verdi, 75, had his requiem in memory of Gioachino Rossini, composed in 1869, premiered after 19 years.

Richard Strauss, 24, (11 June 1864 – 8 Sep 1949, aged 85.2, German composer) wrote the symphonic poem, *Don Juan*, which brings him fame.

In 1865, cultural and scientific personalities such as Constantin Esarcu, V. A. Urechia, and Nicolae Crețulescu founded the Romanian Atheneum Cultural Society. To serve its purposes, the Romanian Athenaeum, a building dedicated to art and science, would be erected in Bucharest. The building was designed by the French architect Albert Galleron, built on a property that had belonged to the Văcărescu family, and inaugurated 23 years later, in 1888.

1889 – July - Verdi, 75.7, received from Boito, 47.4, the draft libretto for Falstaff, after Verdi had just read Shakespeare's play *The Merry Wives of Windsor*. Boito began work some time ago on this libretto, based on *The Merry Wives of Windsor*, with additional material taken from *Henry IV, Part 1* and *Part 2*. Verdi: responded: "Benissimo! Benissimo!", and began working on Falstaff. Boito also informed Verdi about Toscanini's (22.4) ability to interpret Verdi's scores.

Beniamino Gigli: 1890 – 1957, 67

1890 – 20 March - **Beniamino Gigli** was born (20 March 1890 – 30 November 1957, aged 67.6). He was an Italian opera singer. He is one of the greatest tenors. In 1914, he, 24, won first prize in an international singing competition in Parma. His operatic debut came on 15 October 1914, when he, 24.6, played Enzo in Amilcare Ponchielli's La Gioconda in Rovigo, following which he was in great demand. Gigli made many important debuts in quick succession, and always in Mefistofele: Teatro Massimo in Palermo (31 March 1915, age 25), Teatro di San Carlo in Naples (26 December 1915, age 25.7), Teatro Costanzi di Roma (26 December 1916, age 26.7), La Scala, Milan (19 November 1918, age 28.6) and finally the Metropolitan Opera, New York (26 November 1920, age 30.6). Two other great Italian tenors present on the roster of Met singers during the 1920s also happened to be Gigli's chief contemporary rivals for tenor supremacy, Giovanni Martinelli and Giacomo Lauri-Volpi.

Some of the roles with which Gigli became associated included Edgardo in Donizetti's Lucia di Lammermoor, Rodolfo in Giacomo Puccini's La Bohème, and the title role in Umberto Giordano's Andrea Chénier, both of which he would later record in full. Gigli rose to true international prominence after the death of the greatest tenor Enrico Caruso in 1921. He, 31, was often called "Caruso Secondo". Gigli left the Met in 1932, age 42, apparently after refusing to take a pay cut. After leaving the Met, Gigli returned again to Italy, and sang in houses there, elsewhere in Europe, and in South America. In addition to his stage performances, Gigli appeared as an actor in over twenty films from 1935 (age 45) to 1953 (age 63). Before his retirement in 1955, Gigli, 65, undertook an exhausting world tour of farewell concerts. Many of Gigli's recordings, including complete operas with Maria Caniglia, Rina Gigli, Licia Albanese and Toti dal Monte, have been reissued on CD. Gigli recordings date back to the 1920s.

- 27 November –Verdi was 77.1 when Emanuele Muzio died (24 August 1821 – 27 Nov 1890 in Paris, aged 69.2, Italian composer, conductor and vocal teacher. He was a lifelong friend, and the only student of Giuseppe Verdi).

- Tchaikovsky's (age 50) *The Sleeping Beauty* debuted in St. Petersburg.

1891 - Carnegie Hall opened in New York.

1893 – 9 February - Verdi, 79.3, had his last of his 28 operas, Falstaff, premiered at Teatro Alla Scala in Milano, Boito, 50.9, wrote the libretto, based on Shakespeare's *The Merry Wives of Windsor,* with additional material taken from *Henry IV, Part 1* and *Part 2.*

For the first night, official ticket prices were thirty times higher than usual. Royalty, aristocracy, critics, and leading figures from the arts all over Europe were present. The performance was a huge success; numbers were encored, and at the end the applause for Verdi and the cast lasted an hour. That was followed by a tumultuous welcome when the composer, his wife and Boito arrived at the Grand Hotel et de Milan (400 m northeast of La Scala, on Via Manzoni, 29, opened 30 years before, in 1863).

May - Verdi, 79.6, had his opera Falstaff presented at Teatro Costanzi in Roma.

In Roma, crowds of well-wishers at the railway station initially forced Verdi to take refuge in a toolshed. He witnessed the performance from the Royal Box, at the side of King Umberto I, 48.9, (14 March 1844, in Torino, Kingdom of Sardinia – 29 July 1900 in Monza, Kingdom of Italy, aged 56.3, King of Italy for 22.5 years: 9 Jan 1878 – 29 July 1900), and the Queen Margherita di Savoia, 41.3, (20 Nov 1851 in Torino, Kingdom of Sardinia – 4 Jan 1926 in Bordighera, Italia, aged 74.1).

Antonin Dvorak (8 Sep 1841 – 1 May 1904, aged 62.6, Czech composer) composed his best and most popular work, *From the New World.*

Viorica Ursuleac: 1894 – 1985, 91

1894 – 26 March - **Viorica Ursuleac** was born (26 March 1894, Chernivtsi, Romania (now in Ukraine) – 22 October 1985,

Ehrwald in Tyrol, Austria, aged 91.6). She was a Romanian operatic soprano. Following training in Vienna, she made her operatic debut in Zagreb (Agram), as Charlotte in Massenet's Werther, in 1922, age 28. The soprano then appeared at the Vienna Volksoper (1924 – 1926 (age 32)), Frankfurt Opera (1926 – 1930 (age 36)), Vienna State Opera (1930 – 1935 (age 41)), Berlin State Opera (1935 – 1937 (age 43)), and Bavarian State Opera (1937 – 1944 (age 50)). She married the Austrian conductor Clemens Krauss in Frankfurt during her time there (age 34).

She was Richard Strauss's favorite soprano. She sang in the world premieres of four of his operas: Arabella (1933 (age 39)), Friedenstag (which was dedicated to Ursuleac, 44, and Krauss, 1938), Capriccio (1942 (age 48)), and the public dress-rehearsal of Die Liebe der Danae (1944 (age 50)).

She appeared at the Salzburg Festival (1930 – 1934 and 1942 – 1943), and in one season at The Royal Opera Covent Garden (1934 (age 40)) where she sang also Arabella (her favorite role). She also appeared as Desdemona in Verdi's Otello at the Royal Opera, with Lauritz Melchior in the name part, and Sir Thomas Beecham conducting.

Ursuleac sang at La Scala in Richard Strauss's Die Frau ohne Schatten (as the Empress), and Elektra (as Chrysothemis), Mozart's Così fan tutte, and Wagner's Die Walküre (as Sieglinde). Her only American appearances were at the Teatro Colón in Buenos Aires, in 1948, age 54. Also in her repertory were the Countess Almaviva (The Marriage of Figaro), Donna Elvira (Don Giovanni), Leonore (Fidelio), Senta (Der fliegende Holländer, with Hans Hotter), Amelia Grimaldi (Simon Boccanegra), Amelia (Un ballo in maschera), Leonora (La forza del destino), Élisabeth de Valois (Don Carlos), Tosca, Minnie (La fanciulla del West), Turandot (opposite Erna Berger's Liù), Der Rosenkavalier, Ariadne auf Naxos (first as the Composer, then as Ariadne), Die ägyptische Helena, etc.

She, 59, gave her farewell in 1953, in Wiesbaden, in Der Rosenkavalier. Her husband Clemens Krauss died in 1954, when she was 60. Ursuleac, 70, was appointed professor at the Salzburg Mozarteum in 1964.

Ursuleac did many live recordings, singing especially Strauss.

1895 – Verdi, 82, started planning, building and endowing a rest-home for retired musicians in Milan, the Casa di Riposo per Musicisti, and building a hospital at Villanova sull'Arda, close to Busseto.

Rome: Inside the Amphitheatrum Flavium (Colosseum, 80 AD), close to the north entrance.

Traian Grozăvescu: 1895 – 1927, 31

- 21 November - **Traian Grozăvescu** was born (21 November 1895, Lugoj, Austro-Hungary, now Romania – 14 February 1927, aged 31.2). He was a Romanian operatic tenor. In 1922, age 27, following a disagreement with the Cluj Opera, he left for Vienna, and sang at the Vienna State Opera, as well as at the Hungarian State Opera House, and the Berlin State Opera, achieving great success.

1897 – 21 August - Verdi, 83.9, completed his last composition, a setting of the traditional Latin text Stabat Mater. This was the last of four sacred works that Verdi composed, Quattro Pezzi Sacri, which are often performed together or separately.

14 November - Verdi was 84.1 when his wife Giuseppina passed (8 Sep 1815 – 14 Nov 1897, aged 82.2, operatic soprano of great renown).

Teresa Stolz, 63.4, remained a companion of Verdi until his death.

1898 – 7 April - Verdi, 84.5, had the first performance of the Quattro Pezzi Sacri at the Grande Opéra, Paris. The four works are: Ave Maria for mixed chorus; Stabat Mater for mixed chorus and orchestra; Laudi alla Vergine Maria for female chorus; and Te Deum for double chorus and orchestra.

Arturo Toscanini, 31, consulted Verdi personally about Verdi's *Te Deum.*

1900 – 29 July – Verdi was 86.8 when King Umberto I died (14 March 1844, in Torino, Kingdom of Sardinia – 29 July 1900 in Monza, Kingdom of Italy, aged 56.3, King of Italy for 22.5 years: 9 Jan 1878 – 29 July 1900).

Verdi he was deeply saddened by the death of King Umberto I, whom he met in Roma 7 years before, and sketched a setting of a poem in his memory, but was unable to complete it.

Jean Sibelius's, 35, (8 December 1865 – 20 September 1957, aged 91.7, Finnish composer) Finlandia premiered in Helsinki.

1901 – 21 January – Verdi, 87.2, had a stroke, while staying at the Grand Hotel et de Milan. He gradually grew feebler over the next days, during which Teresa Stolz, 66.5, cared for him

27 January – Verdi died at the age of 87 years, 3 months and 18 days, while staying at the Grand Hotel et de Milan, six days after the stroke.

Verdi was initially buried in Milan's Cimitero Monumental.

February - A month later, his body was moved to the crypt of the Casa di Riposo. On this occasion, "Va, pensiero" from *Nabucco* was conducted by Arturo Toscanini, 33.9, with a chorus of 820 singers. A huge crowd was in attendance, estimated at 300,000. Arturo Toscanini conducted the vast forces of combined orchestras and choirs, composed of musicians from throughout Italy, at the state funeral for Verdi in Milan. To date, it remains the largest public assembly of any event in the history of Italy.

Verdi came to lead the Italian opera scene after the era of Gioachino Rossini, Gaetano Donizetti, and Vincenzo Bellini. By his 30s, he had become one of the pre-eminent opera composers in history.

Petre Ştefănescu Goangă: 1902 – 1973, 71

1902 – 3 March - **Petre Ştefănescu Goangă** was born (3 March 1902, Brăila, Romania – 5 September 1973, Bucharest, aged 71.5). He was a Romanian baritone and teacher, who studied in Paris, and sang in many European countries. At the age of 22 in 1924, he debuted on the stage of the Bordeaux Opera in the role of 'Mefisto' in Faust by Charles Gounod. The moment of the transition from the bass to the baritone takes place in 1926, on the stage of the opera in Toulouse, where he, 24, interprets Tonio in Pagliacci by Ruggiero Leoncavallo. Between 1928 and 1931, he (26 – 29) reached the peak of the lyrical career, at the Theater Royal from Monnaie, Brussels, Rouen, Amsterdam, Antwerp, Rotterdam, Gand, Hague, Barcelona, Bruges and Nomur. Between 1932 and 1934 he (30 – 32) was a soloist at the Romanian Opera in Cluj, performing: Tosca, Pagliacci, Cavalleria Rusticana, Il Trovatore, La Traviata, Rigoletto. After 1949 he, 47, became a teacher at the singing department of the Bucharest Conservatory.

- 14 July – The original Campanile della Basilica di San Marco (1156 – 1173, last restored in 1514), in Venezia, collapsed.

Claude Debussy (22 August 1862 – 25 March 1918, aged 55.6, French composer) composed *Pelléas and Mélisande* for the Opéra Comique in Paris.

1904 - The London Symphony Orchestra was established.

1910 - **Igor Stravinsky,** 28, (17 June 1882 – 6 April 1971, aged 88.8, Russian composer) completes *The Firebird* for **Sergei Diaghilev**'s, 38, (31 March 1872, Russia – 19 August 1929, Venice, Italy, aged 57.4) Ballets Russes.

Ion Dacian: 1911 – 1981, 70

1911 - Strauss's, 47, *Der Rosenkavalier* premieres in Dresden.

11 October - **Ion Dacian** was born (11 October 1911 – 8 December 1981, Bucharest, aged 70.1). He was a Romanian tenor known especially as a light opera singer.

Venice: Basilica di San Marco (left), Palazzo Ducale (center), Palazzo delle Prigioni (right).

Tito Gobbi: 1913 – 1984, 70

1913 – 24 October - **Tito Gobbi** was born (24 October 1913 – 5 March 1984, aged 70.3). He was an Italian operatic baritone with an international reputation. He made his operatic debut in Gubbio in 1935, age 22, as Count Rodolfo in Bellini's La sonnambula, and quickly appeared in Italy's major opera houses. By the time he retired in 1979, age 66, he had acquired a repertoire of almost 100 operatic roles. They ranged from Mozart's mid-range baritone roles through Rossini's Barber through Donizetti and the standard Verdi and Puccini baritone roles. He had a worldwide career as operatic baritone, appearing in (or recording the singing role) for over 25 films and, from the mid-1960s onward, was the stage director for about ten different operas, which were given close to 35 productions throughout Europe and North America, including a significant number in Chicago for the Lyric Opera of Chicago. Accompanying Gobbi on the piano at his first audition was Tilde De Rensis, daughter of musicologist Raphael De Rensis. In 1937, age 24, she became his wife. Gobbi and Tilda had a daughter, Cecilia, who now runs the "Associazione Musicale Tito Gobbi". He was also the brother-in-law of one of his famous colleagues at Covent Garden, the Bulgarian-born bass, Boris Christoff.

Mario Del Monaco: 1915 – 1982, 67

1915 – 27 July - **Mario Del Monaco** was born (27 July 1915 – 16 October 1982, aged 67.2). He was an Italian operatic tenor. As a young boy he studied the violin, but had a passion for singing. He graduated from the Rossini Conservatory at Pesaro, where he first met and sang with Renata Tebaldi, 6.5 years younger than him (1 Feb 1922 – 19 Dec 2004, aged 82.9), with whom he would form something of an operatic team of the 1950s. Del Monaco's debut was on 31 December 1940, age 25.4, as Pinkerton at the Puccini Theater in Milan. He sang in Italy during the Second World War and married, in 1941, age 26, Rina Filipini. In 1946, he, 31, appeared at London's Royal Opera House, Covent Garden, for the first time.

Del Monaco sang at the New York Metropolitan Opera from 1951 (age 36) to 1959 (age 44), enjoying particular success in dramatic Verdi parts such as Radamès. He soon established himself as one of the great Italian tenor superstars, who reached the peak of their fame in the 1950s and '60s, together with Giuseppe Di Stefano. Del Monaco sang a number of roles with great acclaim: Verdi's Otello, Canio in Pagliacci (Leoncavallo), Radames in Aida (Verdi), Don Jose in Carmen (Bizet), Chenier in Andrea Chénier (Giordano), Manrico in Il trovatore (Verdi), Samson in Samson and Delilah (Saint-Saëns), and Don Alvaro in La forza del destino (Verdi).

Del Monaco made his first recordings in Milan in 1948 for HMV. Later, he was partnered by Renata Tebaldi in a long series of Verdi and Puccini operas recorded for Decca. On the same label was his 1969, age 54, recording of Giordano's Fedora, with Magda Olivero and Tito Gobbi, 56. In 1975 Del Monaco, 60, retired from the stage.

Zenaida Pally: 1919 – 1997, 78

1919 – 10 June - **Zenaida Pally** was born (10 June 1919 Soroca, Romania - 26 June 1997, Saarbrücken, Germany, aged 78). She was a Romanian mezzo-soprano of international fame. She graduated from three faculties between 1940 (age 21) and 1945 (age 26): The Commercial Faculty, Belle Arte Academy, and the Music Conservatory. She debuted as a soloist of the Bucharest Opera and

Ballet Theater in May 1945, age 26, in the role of Amneris in Aida by Giuseppe Verdi. Shortly after, she went on a tour in Budapest, where she sang with Petre Ștefănescu-Goangă, 17 years older than her. She performed a large number of roles, and made many tours in Europe, as well as recordings for the Romanian Broadcasting Company. In 1974 she, 55, emigrated to Germany, where she continued her career as a soloist at Saarbrücken until 1988, age 69.

Nicola Rossi-Lemeni: 1920 – 1991, 70

1920 – 6 November - **Nicola Rossi-Lemeni** was born (6 November 1920, Istanbul, Turkey – 12 March 1991, Bloomington, USA, aged 70.3). He was a basso opera singer of mixed Italian-Russian parentage, being the son of an Italian colonel and a Russian mother. In his prime he was one of the most respected bassos in Italy. He was also a prize-winning poet and a painter.

The basso made his debut as Varlaam in Boris Godunov at La Fenice, Venice, in 1946, age 26. He sang at the Teatro alla Scala from 1947 (age 27) to 1960 (age 40), the Teatro Colón (1949, age 29) and Covent Garden (1952, age 32). He appeared at the Metropolitan Opera, opening the 1953/54 season (age 33), in Faust, followed by the title roles of Don Giovanni and Boris Godunov.

He sang Don Giovanni to open the newly established Lyric Theatre of Chicago in February 1954, aged 33.2, (renamed two years later as Lyric Opera of Chicago), and returned that fall for Norma with Callas in her American debut, and Basilio in The Barber of Seville. The following season he appeared in Puritani with Callas, Boheme with Tebaldi, Faust with Bjoerling, Elisir with Carteri, and L'amore dei tre re with Kirsten. Rossi-Lemeni was married to Romanian soprano Virginia Zeani. Among his recordings are Don Carlos (with Mirto Picchi, 1951, age 31), The Barber of Seville (with de los Ángeles, 1952, age 32), and—opposite Maria Callas—I puritani (1953, age 33), Norma (1954, age 34), Il turco in Italia (1954) and La forza del destino (1954). He was then featured in two recordings of La serva padrona, the first (1955, age 35) conducted by Carlo Maria Giulini, the second (1959, age 39) alongside Zeani. In 1952, he, 32, recorded excerpts from Boris Godunov with Leopold

Stokowski, and the San Francisco Symphony, for RCA Victor, which have been reissued on CD.

Boston Harbor (1614), Rowes Wharf (1666, 1764, 1987): the bow (front) and the starboard (right side) of the yacht Odyssey.

Giuseppe Di Stefano: 1921 – 2008, 86

1921 – 24 July - **Giuseppe Di Stefano** was born (24 July 1921, Motta Sant'Anastasia, a village near Catania, Sicily – 3 March 2008, aged 86.6). He was an Italian operatic tenor, one of the most beautiful voices. Luciano Pavarotti said he modeled himself after Di Stefano, and he was also the tenor who most inspired José Carreras. Di Stefano was educated at a Jesuit seminary, and briefly contemplated entering the priesthood. After briefly taking lessons from the Swiss tenor Hugues Cuénod, Di Stefano made his operatic debut in 1946, age 25, in Reggio Emilia as Des Grieux in Massenet's Manon, the role in which he made his La Scala debut, age 26, the following year. He made his New York debut at the Metropolitan Opera in February 1948, age 27, as the Duke of Mantua in Verdi's Rigoletto, after singing the role in Riccione with Hjördis Schymberg in August of the previous year, age 26. He went on to perform regularly in New York for many years. In 1957, Di Stefano, 36, made his British debut at the Edinburgh Festival as Nemorino in L'elisir d'amore, and his Royal Opera House, Covent Garden, debut in 1961, age 40, as Cavaradossi in Tosca. In his Metropolitan Opera radio broadcast debut in Faust, he attacked the high Do (C) in "Salut! demeure" forte, and then had a diminuendo to a pianissimo, which was much admired, especially by Sir Rudolf Bing.

In 1953 Walter Legge, leader of EMI's classical wing, wanted a tenor to record all the popular Italian operas with Maria Callas, 29.6, and chose Di Stefano, 32. Among their recording achievements was the famous 1953 studio recording of Tosca under Victor de Sabata. The two also performed together on stage frequently, from 1951 (he 30, she 27.6) in South America to the end of 1957 (he 36.4, she 34) in Un ballo in maschera at La Scala, the last time the two collaborated in an opera. He, 34, sang Alfredo in the famous Visconti production of La Traviata in 1955 at La Scala, as well as Edgardo in Lucia under Herbert von Karajan at La Scala, Berlin and Vienna. In 1973, Di Stefano, 52, and Maria Callas, 49.6, went together for a recital tour that ended in 1974. Di Stefano continued to sing successfully, and his final operatic role was as the Emperor in Turandot, in July 1992, age 71.

Renata Tebaldi: 1922 – 2004, 82

1922 – 1 February - **Renata Ersilia Clotilde Tebaldi** was born (1 February 1922, Pesaro, Italy – 19 December 2004, San Marino, aged 82.9). She was an Italian lirico-spinto soprano. She was admitted to the conservatory at the age of 17, in 1939.
Tebaldi made her stage debut as Elena in Boito's Mefistofele in Rovigo in 1944 (age 22), and performed in Parma in La bohème, L'amico Fritz and Andrea Chénier. In 1946 she, 24, made her debut as Desdemona alongside Francesco Merli as Otello in Trieste.
Her major breakthrough came in 1946, when she, 24, auditioned for Arturo Toscanini, 79, (25 March 1867 – 16 Jan 1957, aged 89.8). Toscanini was favorably impressed, calling her "voce d'angelo" (voice of an angel). Tebaldi made her La Scala debut that year at the concert which marked the reopening of the theatre after World War II. She sang the "Prayer" ("Dal tuo stellato soglio") from Rossini's biblical opera, Mosè in Egitto, as well as the soprano part in Verdi's Te Deum. She was given the operatic roles of Margherita and Elena in Mefistofele, and Elsa in Lohengrin in 1946. The following year, she, 25, appeared in La Bohème, and as Eva in Die Meistersinger. Toscanini encouraged her to sing the role of Aida and invited her to rehearse the role in his studio. She was of the opinion that the role of Aida was reserved for a dramatic soprano, but Toscanini convinced her, and she made her role debut at La Scala in 1950, age 28, alongside Mario del Monaco, 35, and Fedora Barbieri, 30, in a performance conducted by Antonino Votto. This was the greatest success in her still young career, and was to launch her international career. Her, 31, voice was used for Sophia Loren's, 19, (20 Sep 1934 – now 84) singing in the film version of Aida (1953).
She, 28, went on a concert tour with the La Scala ensemble in 1950, first to the Edinburgh Festival, and then on to London, where she made her debut as Desdemona in two performances of Otello at Covent Garden, and in the Verdi Requiem, both conducted by Victor de Sabata. Tebaldi made her American debut in 1950 as Aida at the San Francisco Opera; her Metropolitan Opera debut took place on 31 January 1955 (age 33), as Desdemona, with Mario Del Monaco's, 40, Otello. For some twenty years, she made the Met the focus of her activities. She sang there some 270 times in La bohème,

Madama Butterfly, Tosca, Manon Lescaut, La fanciulla del West, Otello, La forza del destino, Simon Boccanegra, Falstaff, Andrea Chénier, Adriana Lecouvreur, La Gioconda, and Violetta in a production of La Traviata created specially for her. She, 46, was Adriana Lecouvreur on the night Placido Domingo, 27, (21 Jan 1941 – now 78) made his Met debut in 1968. She, 50.9, made her last appearance there as Desdemona in Otello, on 8 January 1973, the same role in which she had made her Met debut almost 18 years earlier. By the end of her career, Tebaldi had sung in 1,262 performances, 1,048 complete operas, and 214 concerts. Tebaldi never married. She had a short relationship with Nicola Rossi-Lemeni (1.2 years older than her), and a longer one with Arturo Basile (8 years older than her, Italian conductor). Tebaldi retired from the stage in 1973 (age 50.9), and from the concert hall in 1976 (age 54). She spent the majority of her last years in Milan and San Marino.

Italy, Naples (Napoli, 1500 BC), from Via Francesco Caracciolo looking north: Chalet del Mare restaurant on the shore of the Tyrrhenian Sea, and buildings from the Chiaia sector of Napoli.

Maria Callas: 1923 -1977, 53

1923 – 2 December - **Maria Callas** was born (2 December 1923, New York City, USA – 16 September 1977, of heart attack, Paris, France, aged 53.7). She was an American-born Greek soprano. Her repertoire ranged from classical opera of Donizetti, Bellini and Rossini and further, to the works of Verdi and Puccini; and, others. Born in New York City to Greek immigrant parents, she was raised mostly by her mother, who moved back to Greece. Maria received her musical education in Athens, Greece at age 13, in 1936, and later established her career in Italy. She had near-sightedness that left her nearly blind onstage. She was christened Maria Anna Cecilia Sofia Kalogeropoulos, and her father had shortened the surname Kalogeropoulos first to "Kalos" and subsequently to "Callas" in order to make it more manageable. After several appearances as a student, Callas began appearing in secondary roles at the Greek National Opera. Callas made her professional debut in February 1941, age 17.1, in the small role of Beatrice in Franz von Suppé's Boccaccio. Callas sang the role of Santuzza in Cavalleria Rusticana again and followed it with O Protomastoras (Manolis Kalomiris) at the ancient Odeon of Herodes Atticus theatre at the foot of the Acropolis. During August and September 1944, Callas, 20.7, performed the role of Leonore in a Greek language production of Fidelio, again at the Odeon of Herodes Atticus. When she left Greece on September 14, 1945, age 21.8, Callas had given 56 performances in seven operas, and had appeared in around 20 recitals. Basso Nicola Rossi-Lemeni, 3 years older than her, was aware that Tullio Serafin was looking for a dramatic soprano to cast as La Gioconda at the Arena di Verona. Subsequently he recommended Callas to retired tenor and impresario Giovanni Zenatello. It was in this role that Callas made her Italian debut. Upon her arrival in Verona, Callas met Giovanni Battista Meneghini (11 Jan 1896 – 21 Jan 1981, aged 85), 27.9 years older, wealthy industrialist, who began courting her. They married in 1949 (she 25.3, he 53.2, and he assumed control of her career for 10 years, until November 1959, when Callas, 35.9, left him, 63.8, because of an affair with Onassis. It was Meneghini's love and support that gave

Callas the time needed to establish herself in Italy, and throughout the prime of her career, she went by the name of Maria Meneghini Callas. After La Gioconda, Callas had no further offers, and when the Italian conductor Tullio Serafin, 45.2 years older than her, (1 Sep 1878 – 2 Feb 1968, aged 89.4), looking for someone to sing Isolde, called on her, she told him that she already knew the score, even though she had looked at only the first act, out of curiosity, while at the conservatory. Serafin immediately cast her in the role, and thereafter served as Callas's mentor and supporter. The great turning point in Callas's career occurred in Venice in 1949. She, 25.5, was engaged to sing the role of Brünnhilde in Die Walküre at the Teatro la Fenice, when Margherita Carosio, who was engaged to sing Elvira in I puritani in the same theatre, fell ill. Unable to find a replacement for Carosio, Serafin, 70.7, told Callas that she would be singing Elvira in six days; when Callas protested that she not only did not know the role, but also had three more Brünnhildes to sing, he told her "I guarantee that you can". This initial incursion into the bel canto repertoire changed the course of Callas's career, and set her on a path leading to Lucia di Lammermoor, La Traviata, Armida, La sonnambula, Il pirata, Il turco in Italia, Medea, and Anna Bolena. As with I puritani, Callas learned and performed Cherubini's Medea, Giordano's Andrea Chénier, and Rossini's Armida on a few days' notice. In a 1952 RAI recital she, 28.5, opened with Lady Macbeth's "letter scene", followed by the "Mad Scene" from Lucia di Lammermoor, then Abigaille's recitative and aria from Nabucco, finishing with the "Bell Song" from Lakmé capped by a ringing high Mi (E) in alt (Mi6). Callas made her official debut at La Scala in Verdi's I vespri siciliani on opening night in December 1951, age 28, and this theatre became her artistic home throughout the 1950s. The night of the day she married Meneghini in Verona, she sailed for Argentina to sing at the Teatro Colón in Buenos Aires. Callas, 25.4, made her South American debut in Buenos Aires on May 20, 1949, during the European summer opera recess. Aida, Turandot and Norma roles were directed by Serafin, 70.6, with Mario Del Monaco, 33.8, (27 July 1915 – 16 Oct 1982, aged 67.2), Fedora Barbieri, 28.9, (4 June 1920 – 4 March 2003, aged 82.7), and Nicola Rossi-Lemeni, 28.5. During 1953 and early 1954, she, 30, lost over 35 kg (from 91 kg to 56 kg, hight 1.74 m (normal weight 72 kg)). Her debut in the United States was five years later in Chicago in

1954, age 30.4, in Norma, at the Lyric Opera of Chicago. Her Metropolitan Opera debut, opening the Met's 72nd season on 29 October 1956, age 32.9, was again with Norma. On 21 November 1957, Callas, 33.9, gave a concert to inaugurate the Dallas Civic Opera. In 1958, she, 34.7, gave a performance as Violetta in La Traviata. She, 41.2, returned to the Met in 1965 to sing the title role in two performances as Tosca with Franco Corelli as Cavaradossi for one performance (19 March 1965), and Richard Tucker (25 March 1965) with Tito Gobbi as Scarpia for her final performances at the Met. In 1952, she, 28.5, made her London debut at the Royal Opera House in Norma, with veteran mezzo-soprano Ebe Stignani as Adalgisa, a performance which survives on record, and also features the 2.9 years younger Joan Sutherland, 25.6, in the small role of Clotilde. She returned to the Royal Opera House in 1953, 1957, 1958, 1959, and 1964 to 1965. It was at the Royal Opera House where, on 5 July 1965, Callas, 41.6 ended her stage career in the role of Tosca, in a production designed and mounted by Franco Zeffirelli, 42.4, 9.7 months older than her, (born 12 Feb 1923, now (2019) 96 years), and featuring her friend and colleague Tito Gobbi, 51.7, (24 Oct 1913 – 5 March 1984, aged 70.4). In 1957, while still married to husband Giovanni Battista Meneghini, 61.4, Callas, 33.5, was introduced to Greek shipping magnate Aristotle Onassis, 51.4, (20 Jan 1906 – 15 March 1975, aged 69.1) at a party given in her honor by Elsa Maxwell, after a performance in Donizetti's Anna Bolena. The affair that followed received much publicity, and in November 1959, Callas, 35.9, left her husband, 63.8. The affair ended in 1968, when Onassis, 62.8, left Callas, 44.9, in favor of Jacqueline Kennedy, 39.3, (28 July 1929 – 19 May 1994, aged 64.8). In 1973, Di Stefano, 52, and Maria Callas, 49.6, went together for a recital tour that ended in 1974. Callas spent her last years living largely in isolation in Paris. In 2014, Warner Classics (formerly EMI Classics) released the Maria Callas Remastered Edition, consisting of her complete studio recordings, totaling 39 albums, in a boxed set remastered at Abbey Road Studios in 24-bit/96 kHz digital sound from original master tapes.

Italy, Santuario de la Santissima Vergine del Rosario (center, 1925), in the downtown of the modern Pompei (founded 650 BC).

Elena Cernei: 1924 – 2000, 76

1924 – 1 March - **Elena Cernei** was born (1 March 1924, Bairamcea near Cetatea Albă, Romania (now in Ukraine) – 27 November 2000, aged 76.7). She was a Romanian operatic mezzo-soprano, musicologist, and voice teacher. During her 25-year career as an opera singer, she sang in leading opera houses in both Europe and North America. She studied singing at the Ciprian Porumbescu Conservatory in Bucharest, with Constantin Stroescu from 1951 (age 27) to 1955 (age 31). During that period, she also sang as a soloist with the George Enescu Philharmonic Orchestra, and at the Romanian National Opera. She continued to sing with the Romanian National Opera from 1952 to 1977, age 53, as well as touring Europe and North America starting in the mid-1960s, age 41. Outside of Romania she sang at La Scala, the New York Metropolitan Opera, Opéra National de Paris, Bolshoi Theatre, Gran Teatre del Liceu in Barcelona, La Monnaie in Brussels, and the Palacio de Bellas Artes in Mexico City. She made her Metropolitan Opera debut on 17 March 1965, age 41, as Dalila in Samson et Dalila. She performed with the company from 1965 to 1968 (age 44) where in addition to Dalila, she sang Amneris in Aida, Maddalena in Rigoletto, Princess di Bouillon in Adriana Lecouvreur, and the title role in Carmen. Other roles which she sang during her career included: Azucena in Il trovatore, Clytemnestra in Iphigénie en Aulide, Arsace in Semiramide, Rosina in The Barber of Seville, Ulrica in Un ballo in maschera, Princess Eboli in Don Carlos, Laura and La Cieca in La Gioconda, Cherubino in Le nozze di Figaro, Jocaste in Œdipe, and Orfeo in Orfeo ed Euridice.

She settled in Rome with her husband, the physician and musicologist Stephan Poen, and, in her later years, taught voice and served on the juries of several singing competitions in Italy and Romania. Many of her performances in Romania were recorded on LP by Electrecord. A DVD documentary on her life and career (with extracts from live recordings of her performances) was issued by TVR Media in 2005.

- The Juilliard School opened in New York.

- Maurice Ravel's, 49, (7 March 1875 – 28 December 1937, aged 62.8, French composer, pianist and conductor) *Bolero* opened in Paris.

Dietrich Fischer-Dieskau: 1925 – 2012, 86

1925 – 28 May - **Dietrich Fischer-Dieskau** (28 May 1925 – 18 May 2012, aged 86.9, 10 days before 87). He was a German lyric baritone and conductor of classical music, best known as a singer of Franz Schubert's Lieder, particularly "Winterreise" of which his recordings are still praised half a century after their release. He recorded a very large array of repertoire (spanning centuries), including opera, Lieder and oratorio in German, Italian, English, French, Russian, and Latin. He was one of the best vocal artists of the 20th century. At his peak, he was greatly admired for his interpretive insights and exceptional control of his soft, beautiful voice. Despite the small size of his lyric baritone voice, Fischer-Dieskau also performed and recorded a great many operatic roles. He dominated both the opera and concert platform for over thirty years.

Virginia Zeani: born 1925 (now 93)

- 21 October - **Virginia Zeani** was born (Virginia Zehan; 21 October 1925 (now, in 2019, age 93)). She is a Romanian-born opera singer, who sang leading soprano roles in the opera houses of Europe and North America. She had a repertoire of 69 roles ranging from the heroines in belcanto operas by Rossini and Donizetti, to those of Verdi and Puccini. Zeani made her professional debut in 1948, age 23, as Violetta in La Traviata, which would become one of her signature roles. After her retirement from the stage in 1982, she, 57, became a well-known voice teacher. She was married to the Italian bass Nicola Rossi-Lemeni (6 Nov 1920 – 12 March 1991, aged 70.3) from 1957 (she 32, he 37) until his death in 1991 (she 65.4, he 70.3). A Distinguished Professor Emerita at Indiana University's Jacobs School of Music, where she taught for many years, Zeani lives in Palm Beach County, Florida, USA, and has continued to teach singing privately. When she was 13 a benefactor in the village paid for her to study singing in Bucharest, first with Lucia Anghel, and then with Lydia Lipkowska, who agreed that her voice was that of a soprano and trained her in that repertoire. After World War II ended, she emigrated to Italy and continued her vocal studies in Milan. Zeani made her professional debut as Violetta in La Traviata at the Teatro Duse in Bologna in 1948, age 23, as a last-minute replacement for Margherita Carosio. It was to become her signature role—she sang it 648 times during the course of her career. In 1950 and 1951 she, 26, sang in Egypt in private concerts for King Farouk, as well as in a series of operas in Cairo and Alexandria. She also sang Violetta in Geneva in 1952, age 27, and at London's Stoll Theatre in 1953, age 28. She had made her Florence debut as Elvira in I puritani in 1952, replacing Maria Callas who had withdrawn from the production after two performances. It was during the Puritani performances that she first met her future husband, the Italian bass Nicola Rossi-Lemeni. They met again in 1956, age 31, when she made her La Scala debut as Cleopatra in Handel's Giulio Cesare. Rossi-Lemeni was her Giulio Cesare. He soon proposed and the couple married in 1957 (she 32, he 37). A year later their son Alessandro was born. Zeani and Rossi-Lemeni made their home in Rome, and would appear together in thirteen more operas.

At the start of her career Zeani had specialized in coloratura roles including Lucia in Lucia di Lammermoor, Elvira in I puritani, Gilda in Rigoletto, and Adèle in Le comte Ory. However, in a 1960, age 35, production at the Teatro dell'Opera di Roma she sang all three heroines in The Tales of Hoffmann — Olympia (coloratura soprano), Antonia (lyric soprano), and Giulietta (dramatic soprano). Rossi-Lemeni appeared in the same production playing all four villains — Lindorf, Coppelius, Dr. Miracole, and Dappertutto. From 1970 she, 45, increasingly tested the heavier dramatic soprano roles with great success, notably the title roles in Aida, Tosca, Manon Lescaut, and Fedora. She also sang Elsa in Wagner's Lohengrin and Senta in his Flying Dutchman. Zeani sang 69 roles. She sang in important revivals of Verdi's early and now rarely performed opera Alzira (Rome, 1970) and belcanto operas such as Donizetti's Maria di Rohan (Naples 1965) and Rossini's Otello (Rome, 1968). By the time she had begun her career as a voice teacher in 1980, Zeani, 55, had basically retired from the stage, but she returned in 1982, age 57, for her last opera performance, Mother Marie in Dialogues of the Carmelites at San Francisco Opera. In 1980 Zeani and Rossi-Lemeni settled in the United States, where they had been offered teaching positions at Indiana University's Jacobs School of Music. Zeani retired to West Palm Beach, Florida, in 2004, age 79. In 2017, age 92, the Virginia Zeani Festival had its inaugural season in Mures, Romania. She made very few studio recordings—Tosca, La Traviata and a Verdi–Puccini recital released on LP by the Romanian Electrecord label, and a two-LP set of Donizetti, Bellini, Verdi, and Puccini arias on the Decca label, recorded when Zeani was in her early 30s.

Australia: 80 m southeast of Sydney Opera House, looking northwest to the southeast side of the Opera.

Joan Sutherland: 1926 – 2010, 83

1926 – Over 420 of Vivaldi's compositions thought lost were discovered in a monastery in Piedmont, Italy.

- 7 November - **Dame Joan Alston Sutherland** was born (7 November 1926 – 10 October 2010, aged 83.9). She was an Australian-born coloratura soprano, called La Stupenda. Sutherland was 18 years old when she began studying voice, in 1944, with John and Aida Dickens. She made her concert debut in Sydney, as Dido in a production of Henry Purcell's Dido and Aeneas, in 1947, age 21. In 1951, she, 25, made her stage debut in Eugene Goossens's Judith. She then went to London to further her studies at the Opera School of the Royal College of Music with Clive Carey. She was engaged by the Royal Opera House, Covent Garden, as a utility soprano, and made her debut there on 28 October 1952, age 25.9, as the First Lady in The Magic Flute, followed in November by a few performances as Clotilde in Vincenzo Bellini's opera Norma, with Maria Callas as Norma. In December 1952, she, 26.1, sang her first leading role at the Royal Opera House, Amelia in Un ballo in Maschera by Verdi. Other roles included Agathe in Der Freischütz, the Countess in The Marriage of Figaro, Desdemona in Otello, Gilda in Rigoletto, Eva in Die Meistersinger von Nürnberg, and Pamina in The Magic Flute. Sutherland married Australian conductor and pianist Richard Bonynge on 16 October 1954, age 27.9. Their son, Adam, was born in 1956, age 30. In 1957, she, 31, appeared in Handel's Alcina with the Handel Opera Society, and sang selections from Donizetti's Emilia di Liverpool in a radio broadcast. The following year she sang Donna Anna in Don Giovanni by Mozart, in Vancouver.

In 1959, Sutherland, 33, was invited to sing Lucia di Lammermoor at the Royal Opera House in a production conducted by Tullio Serafin, and staged by Franco Zeffirelli. In 1960, she, 34, recorded the album The Art of the Prima Donna: the double LP set won the Grammy Award for Best Classical Performance – Vocal Soloist in 1962. Sutherland sang Lucia to great acclaim in Paris in 1960 and, in 1961 (age 35), at La Scala and the Metropolitan Opera. In 1960 (age 34), she sang Alcina at La Fenice. Sutherland would soon be praised as La Stupenda in newspapers around the world. Later that year (1960), Sutherland sang Alcina at the Dallas Opera, with which she made her U.S. debut. Her Metropolitan Opera debut took place on 26 November 1961 (age 35), when she sang Lucia. After a total of 223 performances in a number of different operas, her last appearance there was a concert on 12 March 1989, age 62.3. During the 1960s, Sutherland added the heroines of bel canto to her repertoire: Violetta in Verdi's La Traviata, Amina in Bellini's La sonnambula and Elvira in Bellini's I Puritani in 1960 (age 34); the title role in Bellini's Beatrice di Tenda in 1961 (35); Marguerite de Valois in Meyerbeer's Les Huguenots and the title role in Rossini's Semiramide in 1962 (36); Norma in Bellini's Norma and Cleopatra in Handel's Giulio Cesare in 1963 (37). In 1966 she, 40, added Marie in Donizetti's La fille du régiment. In 1965, Sutherland, 39, toured Australia with the Sutherland-Williamson Opera Company. Accompanying her was an 8.9 years young tenor named Luciano Pavarotti, 30. Sutherland's early recordings show her to have a crystal-clear voice and excellent diction. Her last public appearance took place in a gala performance of Die Fledermaus on New Year's Eve, 1990, age 64, at Covent Garden, where she was accompanied by her colleagues Luciano Pavarotti, 55, and the mezzo-soprano Marilyn Horne, 56.

Nicolae Herlea: 1927 – 2014, 86

1927 – 28 August - **Nicolae Herlea** was born (28 August 1927, Bucharest, Romania – 24 February 2014, aged 86.5). He was a highly acclaimed Romanian operatic baritone, particularly associated with the Italian repertory, especially the role of Rossini's Figaro, which he sang around 550 times during his career, and the title role of Rigoletto. Herlea studied at the Bucharest Music Conservatory with Aurelius Costescu-Duca, and later at the Accademia di Santa Cecilia in Rome, with Giorgio Favaretto. In 1951, he, 24, won first prizes in international singing contests in Geneva, Prague, and Brussels. He made his stage debut that same year at the National Opera of Bucharest as Silvio in Pagliacci, quickly establishing himself as the principal baritone there.
In 1958, he, 31, began appearing abroad, particularly at the Bolshoi in Moscow, to where he regularly returned. He also made guest appearances at London's Royal Opera House (1961, age 34), La Scala in Milan (1963, age 36), and the Metropolitan Opera in New York (1964 – 1967, age 37 - 40), and also performed at the Liceo in Barcelona, the Berlin Staatsoper, the Vienna State Opera, the Salzburg Festival, La Monnaie in Brussels, and in the opera houses of Prague and Budapest. He made complete studio recordings of Il Barbiere di Siviglia, Lucia di Lammermoor, Rigoletto, La traviata, La forza del destino, Cavalleria rusticana, "Pagliacci" and Tosca, on labels such as Supraphon and Electrecord.
Herlea also had a successful career in the concert-hall. After he retired, he taught master classes at the Bucharest Conservatory.
He was the President of the Jury of the Hariclea Darclée International Voice Competition.

Roma in 2011: the author (68) is at Pantheon (126 AD) and the Fontana del Pantheon in Piazza della Rotonda. Commissioned in 27 BC by Marcus Agrippa (63 BC -12 BC), and rebuilt by Emperor Hadrian (76–138, Emperor 117-138), in about 126.

Magda Ianculescu: 1929 – 1995, 65

1929 – 30 March - **Magda Ianculescu** was born (30 March 1929, Iași, Romania – 16 March 1995, Bucharest, Romania, aged 65.9, 14 days before 66). She was a Romanian operatic soprano and voice teacher. A leading singer in the Romanian National Opera for many years, she was known for her musicality and vocal technique. Her voice had a wide range and a timbre which many compared to that of Maria Callas.

Magda Ianculescu entered the Bucharest Conservatory of Dramatic Art in 1947, age 18. While in the final years of her studies at the conservatory, she became a member of the Romanian National Opera company in Bucharest. She made her stage debut as Rosina in Rossini's The Barber of Seville, which became one of her signature roles. Between 1953 and 1955 she won singing competitions and went on to perform in Belgium, Italy, France,

Poland, the USSR, Czechoslovakia, Yugoslavia, and other European countries.

Her repertoire included more than 35 principal roles, including Norina in Don Pasquale, Violetta in La Traviata, Donna Elvira in Don Giovanni, Blondchen in The Abduction from the Seraglio, and Susanna in The Marriage of Figaro. She also made many recordings for Romanian National Radio and the Electrecord record company. Ianculescu retired from the stage in 1970, age 41, and from 1969 to 1977 (age 48) she was a professor at the Bucharest Conservatory of Dramatic Art.

Nicolai Ghiaurov: 1929 – 2004, 74

– 13 September - **Nicolai Ghiaurov** was born (13 September 1929, Velingrad, Bulgaria – 2 June 2004, Modena, Italy, aged 74.7). He was a Bulgarian opera singer and one of the most famous basses of the postwar period. He was admired for his powerful, sumptuous voice, and was particularly associated with roles of Mussorgsky and Verdi. Ghiaurov married the Bulgarian pianist Zlatina Mishakova in 1956, age 27, and Italian soprano Mirella Freni in 1978, age 49, and the two singers frequently performed together. They lived in Modena until Ghiaurov's death in 2004 of a heart attack. He was recorded frequently, and his discography includes complete recordings of many of his great stage roles, including Don Giovanni, Don Basilio, Ramfis, Colline, Banco, Gounod's and Boito's Mephistos and Boris Godunov, among many others.

Dan Iordăchescu: 1930 – 2015, 85

1930 – 2 June - **Dan Iordăchescu** was born (2 June 1930, Vânju Mare, Romania – 30 August 2015, aged 85.2). He was a great Romanian baritone, and the father of opera singers Cristina Iordachescu, Irina Iordachescu and Raluca Iordachescu. He performed in 61 countries, and over 300 cities in 262 international tours for over 30 years, and has received many awards. His repertoire included more than 45 principal opera roles (especially by Mozart, Verdi, and Bizet), in over 1080 opera performances, starting with Monteverdi. He also had a successful career in about 1600 concerts, and 31 Festivals in Europe, America and Asia.

USA, New York, from Times Square: W 44th St, looking southeast, with Virgil's Real Barbecue restaurant (center red), MetLife Building (center back).

Anna Moffo: 1932 – 2006, 73

<u>**1932**</u> – 27 June - **Anna Moffo** was born (27 June 1932 – 9 March 2006, aged 73.7). She was an American opera singer, television personality, and dramatic actress. Winning a Fulbright Scholarship to study in Italy, Moffo became popular there after performing leading operatic roles on three RAI television productions in 1956, age 24. She returned to America for her debut at the Lyric Opera of Chicago on 16 October, 1957, age 25.3. In New York, her Metropolitan Opera debut took place on 14 November 1959, age 27.4. She performed at the Met for over seventeen seasons. Although Moffo's earliest recordings were made for EMI Records, she later signed an exclusive contract with RCA

Victor, recording for the company until the late 1970s. In the early 1960s, she, 30, hosted her own show on Italian television, and appeared in several operatic films along with other non-singing roles. In the early 1970s Moffo, 40, extended her international popularity to Germany through operatic performances, TV appearances, and several films, all while continuing her American operatic performances. Moffo suffered a vocal-breakdown from which she never fully recovered. Her final appearance at the Metropolitan Opera was in 1983, age 51.

Marilyn Horne: born 1934 (now 85)

1934 – 16 January - **Marilyn Horne** was born, now (2019) 85. She is an American mezzo-soprano opera singer. For many years, Horne was associated with the Australian soprano Dame Joan Sutherland (7.1 years older than her) in their performances of the bel canto repertoire. They first performed together in a concert version of Vincenzo Bellini's Beatrice di Tenda at The Town Hall in Manhattan in February 1961 (age 27 and 34.1). This performance was so successful, it was repeated twice at Carnegie Hall. In 1965, they (age 31 and 38.1) were paired again in a performance of Rossini's Semiramide with the Opera Company of Boston, and sang in a joint concert on 15 October 1979 (age 45.7 and 52.8), which was telecast as "Live from Lincoln Center". Another of Horne's breakthroughs occurred in 1969 (age 35) during a performance of Rossini's Le siège de Corinthe at La Scala, when Horne received a remarkable mid-act seven-minute ovation. Horne, 36, made her debut at the Metropolitan Opera in 1970 as Adalgisa in Bellini's Norma with Sutherland, 43.1, in the title role. She thereafter appeared regularly at the Met, opening the 1972/1973 (age 39) season as Carmen. A great success there was in Meyerbeer's Le prophète, in John Dexter's production, in 1984 (age 50). Horne, 65, retired from the concert stage in 1999 with a recital at the Chicago Symphony Center.

Mirella Freni: born 1935 (now 84)

1935 – 27 February - **Mirella Freni** was born as Mirella Fregni on 27 February 1935, now (2019) age 84. She is an Italian soprano whose repertoire includes Verdi, Puccini, Mozart and Tchaikovsky. Freni was married for 26 years to the Bulgarian bass Nicolai Ghiaurov (13 September 1929, Velingrad, Bulgaria – 2 June 2004, Modena, Italy, aged 74.7), with whom she performed and recorded. Freni was born into a working-class family in Modena; her mother and tenor Luciano Pavarotti's mother worked together at a cigar factory, and an aunt was the soprano Valentina Bartolomasi. She was a musically gifted child, and when 10 years old, in 1945, sang "Un bel dì vedremo" in a radio competition; the tenor Beniamino Gigli, 55, warned her, however, that she risked ruining her voice, and advised her to give up singing until she was older. She resumed singing at the age of 17, in 1952. Freni made her operatic debut at the Teatro Municipale in her hometown on 3 March 1955, when 20 years old, as Micaëla in Bizet's Carmen. She later married her teacher, the piano player and director Leone Magiera, resuming her career in 1958 when she, 23, performed Mimì in Puccini's La bohème at the Teatro Regio in Turin, and sang in The Netherlands Opera 1959 – 1960 season (age 25). Her international breakthrough came at Glyndebourne, where she sang as Adina in Franco Zeffirelli's staging of Donizetti's L'elisir d'amore; in the Glyndebourne 1960 – 1962 season she, 27, sang the Mozart comic roles of Susanna in Le nozze di Figaro, and Zerlina in Don Giovanni. In 1961, Freni, 26, made her Royal Opera House debut as Nannetta in Verdi's Falstaff, and in 1963, her (age 28) La Scala debut also as Nanetta; Freni went on to become one of Herbert Von Karajan's, 55, (5 April 1908, Austria – 16 July 1989, Austria, aged 81.2) favorite singers, working with him in operas and concerts. In 1965 she, 30, made her Metropolitan Opera debut as Mimì, and later appeared there as Liù in Puccini's Turandot, Marguerite in Faust and Juliette in Roméo et Juliette. The following year she sang Mimì again for her Philadelphia Lyric Opera Company debut, with Flaviano Labò as Rodolfo.

From the early 1970s into the 1980s Freni (35 – 52) sang heavier Verdi roles, particularly Elisabetta in Don Carlos, Desdemona in Otello (with Jon Vickers), Amelia in Simon Boccanegra, Elvira in the Luca Ronconi staging of Ernani, Leonora in La forza del destino, and the title role of Aida performed in Houston in 1987, age 52. She also added the Puccini heroine Manon Lescaut and Tosca to her repertoire. Although Tosca appears to be only on record, she performed 'Manon Lescaut' in the Metropolitan Opera's 1990 season (age 55), and recorded Madama Butterfly and the three roles of Il trittico. Freni, 40, starred in the 1975 film Madama Butterfly with Plácido Domingo, with Karajan, 67, conducting and Jean-Pierre Ponnelle directing, and in 1976 (age 41), played Susanna in the Ponnelle film Le nozze di Figaro, which also featured Dietrich Fischer-Dieskau, 51, Dame Kiri Te Kanawa and Hermann Prey.

In 1978 she, 43, married Nicolai Ghiaurov, 49, one of the leading operatic basses of the post-war period. Together they helped to establish the Centro Universale del Bel Canto in Vignola, where they began giving master classes in 2002 (she 67, he 73). Following Ghiaurov's death in 2004, aged 74.7, Freni, 69.3, continued their work of preserving the bel canto tradition, and currently teaches young singers from around the world. Mirella Freni ended her professional career on stage with The Maid of Orleans at the Washington National Opera on 11 April 2005, performing the teenager Ioanna at age 70.1.

Luciano Pavarotti: 1935 – 2007, 71

1935 — 12 October - **Luciano Pavarotti** was born (12 October 1935, Modena, Italy – 6 September 2007, Modena, Italy, aged 71.9). He was an Italian operatic tenor, who became one of the most successful tenors of all time. He made numerous recordings of complete operas and individual arias. Pavarotti became well known for his televised concerts and media appearances. From the beginning of his professional career as a tenor in 1961 (age 26) in Italy, to his final performance of "Nessun dorma" at the 2006 Winter Olympics in Turin (age 71), Pavarotti was at his best in bel canto operas. He sold over 100 millions of records. As a child, Pavarotti spent seven years in vocal training. Pavarotti's earliest musical influences were his father's collection of record, most of them featuring the popular tenors – Beniamino Gigli, Giovanni Martinelli, Tito Schipa, and Enrico Caruso. Pavarotti's favorite tenor and idol was Giuseppe Di Stefano, and he was also deeply influenced by Mario Lanza. At around the age of nine, in 1944, he began singing with his father in a small local church choir. Pavarotti began the serious study of music in 1954, at the age of 19, with Arrigo Pola, a respected teacher and professional tenor in Modena, who offered to teach him without remuneration. In 1955, he, 20, experienced his first singing success when he was a member of the Corale Rossini, a male voice choir from Modena that also included his father, which won first prize at the International Eisteddfod in Llangollen, Wales. At about this time Pavarotti first met Adua Veroni, and they married in 1961 (age 26). Pavarotti began his career as a tenor in smaller regional Italian opera houses, making his debut as Rodolfo in La Bohème at the Teatro Municipale in Reggio Emilia in April 1961, age 25.5. He made his first international appearance in La Traviata in Belgrade, Yugoslavia. Very early in his career, on 23 February 1963, he, 27.3, debuted at the Vienna State Opera in the same role. In March and April 1963 Vienna saw Pavarotti again as Rodolfo and as Duca di Mantova in Rigoletto. The same year saw his first concert outside Italy when he sang in Dundalk, Ireland for the St Cecilia's Gramophone Society, and his Royal Opera House debut, where he replaced an indisposed Giuseppe Di Stefano as Rodolfo. An early success involved his connection with Joan Sutherland (and her conductor husband, Richard Bonynge), who, in 1963 (age 28), had sought a young tenor taller than herself to take along on her tour to Australia. With his imposing physical presence, Pavarotti proved ideal. The two sang some forty performances over two months, and Pavarotti later credited Sutherland for the breathing technique that would sustain him over his career. Pavarotti made his American début with the Greater Miami Opera in February 1965 (age 29.3), singing in Donizetti's Lucia di Lammermoor, with Joan Sutherland on the stage of the Miami-Dade County Auditorium in Miami. The tenor scheduled to perform that night became ill with no understudy. As Sutherland was traveling with him on tour, she recommended the young Pavarotti as he was well acquainted with the role. Shortly after, on 28 April, Pavarotti, 29.4, made his La Scala debut in the revival of the famous Franco Zeffirelli production of La Bohème, with his childhood friend Mirella Freni singing Mimi and Herbert von Karajan conducting. Karajan had requested the singer's engagement.

After an extended Australian tour, he returned to La Scala, where he added Tebaldo from I Capuleti e i Montecchi to his repertoire on 26 March 1966 (age 30.4), with Giacomo Aragall as Romeo. His first appearance as Tonio in Donizetti's La fille du régiment took place at the Royal Opera House, Covent Garden, on 2 June 1966 (age 30.6). It was his performances of this role that would earn him the title of "King of the High Do (Cs)". He scored another major triumph in Rome on 20 November 1969, age 34.1, when he sang in I Lombardi with Renata Scotto. This was recorded on a private label and widely distributed, as were various recordings of his I Capuleti e i Montecchi, usually with Aragall. Early recordings included a recital of Donizetti (the aria from Don Sebastiano were particularly highly regarded) and Verdi arias, as well as a complete L'elisir d'amore with Sutherland.

His major breakthrough in the United States came on 17 February 1972, age 36.3, in a production of La fille du régiment at New York's Metropolitan Opera, in which he drove the crowd into a frenzy with his nine effortless high Do-s (Cs) in the signature aria. He achieved a record seventeen curtain calls. Pavarotti sang his international recital début at William Jewell College in Liberty, Missouri, on 1 February 1973, 37.3, as part of the college's Fine Arts Program, now known as the Harriman-Jewell Series. Perspiring due to nerves and a lingering cold, the tenor held a handkerchief throughout the début. This became a signature part of his solo performances. He began to give frequent television performances, starting with his performances as Rodolfo (La Bohème) in the first Live from the Met telecast in March 1977, age 41.4, which attracted one of the largest audiences ever for a televised opera. He won many Grammy awards and platinum and gold discs for his performances. In 1979, Pavarotti, 44, returned to the Vienna State Opera after an absence of fourteen years. With Herbert von Karajan conducting, Pavarotti sang Manrico in Il Trovatore. In 1978, he, 43, appeared in a solo recital on Live from Lincoln Center. At the beginning of the 1980s, he, 45, set up The Pavarotti International Voice Competition for young singers, performing with the winners in 1982 (age 47) in excerpts of La bohème and L'elisir d'amore. The second competition, in 1986, age 51, staged excerpts of La Bohème and Un ballo in maschera. To celebrate the 25th anniversary of his career, he brought the winners of the competition to Italy for gala performances of La Bohème in Modena and Genoa, and then to China, where they staged performances of La Bohème in Beijing (Peking). To conclude the visit, Pavarotti performed the inaugural concert in the Great Hall of the People before 10,000 people, receiving a standing ovation for nine effortless high Do (Cs). The third competition in 1989, age 54, again staged performances of L'elisir d'amore and Un ballo in maschera. The winners of the fifth competition accompanied Pavarotti in performances in Philadelphia in 1997, age 62. In the mid-1980s, Pavarotti, 50, returned to two opera houses that had provided him with important breakthroughs, the Vienna State Opera and La Scala. Vienna saw Pavarotti as Rodolfo in La Bohème with Carlos Kleiber conducting and again Mirella Freni was Mimi; as Nemorino in L'elisir d'amore; as Radames in Aida conducted by Lorin Maazel; as Rodolfo in Luisa Miller; and as Gustavo in Un ballo in Maschera, conducted by Claudio Abbado. In 1996, Pavarotti, 61, appeared for the last time at the Staatsoper in Andrea Chénier. In 1985, Pavarotti, 50, sang Radames at La Scala with Maria Chiara in a Luca Ronconi production, conducted by Maazel, recorded on video. His performance of the aria "Celeste Aida" received a two-minute ovation on the opening night. He was reunited with Mirella Freni for the San Francisco Opera production of La Bohème in 1988, age 53, also recorded on video. In 1992, La Scala saw Pavarotti, 57, in a new Zeffirelli production of Don Carlos, conducted by Riccardo Muti. Pavarotti became even better known throughout the world in 1990, age 55, when his rendition of the aria "Nessun dorma" from Giacomo Puccini's Turandot was taken as the theme song of BBC's coverage of the 1990 FIFA World Cup in Italy. The aria achieved high status, became the World Cup soundtrack, and it remained his trademark song. This was followed by the first Three Tenors concert, held on the eve of the 1990 FIFA World Cup Final at the ancient Baths of Caracalla in Rome, with fellow tenors Plácido Domingo and José Carreras, and conductor Zubin Mehta. The performance for the World Cup closing concert captivated a global audience, and it became the biggest selling classical record of all time. Throughout the 1990s, Pavarotti appeared in many well-attended outdoor concerts, including his televised concert in London's Hyde Park, which drew a record attendance of 150,000. In June 1993 (age 57.6), more than 500,000 listeners gathered for his free performance on the Great Lawn of New York's Central Park, while millions more around the world watched on television. The following September, in the shadow of the Eiffel Tower in Paris, he, 57.9, sang for an estimated crowd of 300,000. Pavarotti began his farewell tour in 2004, at the age of 69, performing one last time in old and new locations, after more than four decades on the stage. On 13 March 2004, Pavarotti, 68.4, gave his last performance in an opera at the New York Metropolitan Opera, for which he received a long-standing ovation for his role as the painter Mario Cavaradossi in Giacomo Puccini's Tosca. The author met Pavarotti personally, in a separate room at the New York Metropolitan Opera, where Pavarotti was presenting several of his recordings. On 1 December 2004, he, 69.1, announced a 40-city farewell tour. His last full-scale performance was at the end of a two-month Australasian tour in Taiwan in December 2005, age 70.1. On 10 February 2006, Pavarotti, 70.3, sang "Nessun dorma" at the 2006 Winter Olympics opening ceremony in Turin, Italy, at his final performance. Pavarotti's made one film, a romantic comedy called Yes, Giorgio in 1982 (age 47). He can be seen also in Jean-Pierre Ponnelle's adaptation of Rigoletto for television, released that same year, or in his more than 20 live opera performances taped for television between 1978 (age 43) and 1994 (age 59), most of them with the

Metropolitan Opera, and most available on DVD. He has a very large discography of opera performances.

1939 – Due to the efforts of **Alfredo Casella**, 56, (25 July 1883 – 5 March 1947, aged 63.6, Italian composer, pianist and conductor), some of the recently found compositions were performed at a Vivaldi Week, marking the start of the appreciation of his works in the 20th century. Since 1950, Vivaldi's compositions have enjoyed wide success. A composition by Vivaldi is identified by RV number, which refers to its place in the "Ryom-Verzeichnis" or "Répertoire des oeuvres d'Antonio Vivaldi", a catalog created in the 20th century by the musicologist Peter Ryom (born 31 May 1937 in Copenhagen, Danish musicologist).

USA, Bretton Woods: The fire pit and the southeast side of the Mount Washington Resort (1902).

Plácido Domingo: born 1941 (now 78)

1941 – 21 January - José **Plácido Domingo** Embil was born on 21 January 1941 (now (2019) 78). He is a Spanish opera singer, conductor, and arts administrator. He has recorded over a hundred complete operas and is well known for his versatility, regularly performing in Italian, French, German, Spanish, English and Russian in the most prestigious opera houses in the world. Although primarily a lirico-spinto tenor for most of his career, especially popular for his Cavaradossi, Hoffmann, Don José, and Canio, he quickly moved into more dramatic roles, becoming acclaimed as Otello. In the early 2010s, he, 60, transitioned from the tenor repertory into almost exclusively baritone parts, most notably Simon Boccanegra. He has performed 149 different roles.

He also starred in many cinematically released and televised opera movies, particularly under the direction of Franco Zeffirelli. In 1990, he, 49, began singing with fellow tenors Luciano Pavarotti, 55, and José Carreras, 44, as part of The Three Tenors.

He also increasingly conducts operas and concerts, and is the general director of the Los Angeles Opera in California as of 2017. He was initially the artistic director and later general director of the Washington National Opera from 1996–2011.

Kiri Te Kanawa: born 1944 (now 75)

1944 – 6 March - Dame **Kiri Janette Te Kanawa** was born as Claire Mary Teresa Rawstron, on 6 March 1944 (now (2019) age 75). She is a New Zealand soprano and is associated with the works of Mozart, Strauss, Verdi, Handel and Puccini. Her final performance was in Ballarat, Australia, in October 2016, age 72.6. Te Kanawa was born Claire Mary Teresa Rawstron in Gisborne, New Zealand. She has Māori and European ancestry, but little is known about her birth parents—she was adopted as an infant by Thomas Te Kanawa and his wife, Nell. She was educated at St Mary's College, Auckland, and formally trained in operatic singing by Sister Mary Leo. Te Kanawa began her singing career as a mezzo-soprano but developed into a soprano. Her recording of the

"Nuns' Chorus" from the Strauss operetta Casanova was the first gold record produced in New Zealand. Te Kanawa met Desmond Park on a blind date in London in August 1967, age 23, and they married six weeks later at St Patrick's Cathedral, Auckland. They adopted two children, Antonia (born 1976) and Thomas (born 1979). The couple divorced in 1997, age 53.

She appeared and sang in the 1966, age 22, musical comedy film Don't Let It Get You. In 1966, without an audition, she enrolled at the London Opera Centre to study. She first appeared on stage as the Second Lady in Mozart's The Magic Flute, as well as in performances of Purcell's Dido and Aeneas in December 1968, age 24.7, at the Sadler's Wells Theatre. She also sang the title role in Donizetti's Anna Bolena. In 1969, she, 25, sang Elena in Rossini's La donna del lago at the Camden Festival, and was also offered the role of the Countess in The Marriage of Figaro. Praise for her Idamante in Mozart's Idomeneo led to an offer of a three-year contract as junior principal at the Royal Opera House Covent Garden, where she made her debut as Xenia in Boris Godunov and a Flower Maiden in Parsifal in 1970, age 26.

She appeared at the Santa Fe Opera, a summer opera festival in New Mexico, in the role of the Countess in The Marriage of Figaro, which opened on 30 July 1971, age 27.3. The performance also featured Frederica von Stade in her debut as Cherubino. On 1 December 1971 at Covent Garden, Te Kanawa, 27.7, repeated her Santa Fe performance. This was followed by performances as the Countess at the Opéra National de Lyon and San Francisco Opera in the autumn of 1972, age 28.6. She first sang as Desdemona in Glasgow in 1972, while her Metropolitan Opera début in 1974, age 30, as Desdemona in Otello took place at short notice: she replaced an ill Teresa Stratas at the last minute. Te Kanawa sang at the Glyndebourne Festival in 1973 (age 29), with further débuts in Paris (1975 (age 31), Sydney (1976 (age 32)), Milan (1978 (age 34)), Salzburg (1979 (age 35)), and Vienna (1980 (age 36)). In 1982, she, 38, gave her only stage performances as Tosca in Paris. In 1989, she, 45, added Elisabeth de Valois in Don Carlos to her repertory at Chicago, and, in 1990, age 46, the Countess in Capriccio, sung first at San Francisco and with equal success at Covent Garden, Glyndebourne and the Metropolitan in 1998 (age 54). In subsequent years, Te Kanawa performed at the Lyric Opera of Chicago, Paris Opera, Sydney

Opera House, the Vienna State Opera, La Scala, San Francisco Opera, Munich and Cologne, adding to her repertoire the Mozart roles of Donna Elvira, Pamina, and Fiordiligi to Italian roles such as Mimi in Puccini's La bohème. She played Donna Elvira in Joseph Losey's 1979 (age 35) film adaptation of Don Giovanni.
In 1984, Leonard Bernstein decided to re-record the musical West Side Story, conducting his own music for the first time. Generally known as the "operatic version", it starred Te Kanawa, 40, as Maria, José Carreras as Tony, Tatiana Troyanos as Anita, Kurt Ollmann as Riff, and Marilyn Horne as the offstage voice who sings "Somewhere". Her first appearance in the title role in Arabella was at the Houston Grand Opera in 1977, age 33, followed by the roles of the Marschallin in Der Rosenkavalier and the Countess in Capriccio. In 1981 she, 37, made a recording of The Marriage of Figaro. In April 2010, Te Kanawa, 66, sang the Marschallin in Der Rosenkavalier by Richard Strauss in two performances at the Cologne Opera in Germany. She performed at Haruhisa Handa's inaugural Tokyo Global Concert at Nakano-Zero Hall in Nakano, Tokyo, Japan, on 10 September 2013, age 69.5.

1948 - Columbia Records introduces the 33 1/3 LP ("long playing") record at New York's Waldorf-Astoria Hotel. It allows listeners to enjoy an unprecedented 25 minutes of music per side, compared to the four minutes per side of the standard 78 rpm record. Next year 45 rpm records are sold in the U.S.

René Pape: born 1964 (now 55)

1964 – 4 September - **René Pape** was born on 4 September 1964 (now (2019) age 55). He is a German operatic bass. His maternal grandfather was an operetta tenor. He had his debut with the Berlin Staatsoper Unter den Linden in 1988, age 24, and achieved international recognition in 1991, age 27, when Sir Georg Solti cast him as Sarastro, in a production of Die Zauberflöte, a role he sang again the same year at La Scala in Milan, under Solti's direction. He sang in Haydn's Die Jahreszeiten ("The Seasons") with the Orchestre de Paris and the Chicago Symphony Orchestra, both under Solti (1992, age 28), then Don Fernando (Fidelio), the

Speaker and Sarastro with the Vienna State Opera during the 1992-93 season, King Philip (Don Carlo) in Basle, Switzerland, and had his Bayreuth debut under the baton of James Levine as Fasolt in Das Rheingold in 1994, age 30. The year 1995 saw his (age 31) debut with the Metropolitan Opera, as the Night Watchman in Die Meistersinger, where he has performed practically every year since. Fasolt and King of Egypt (Aida) in 1997, age 33, Escamillo (Carmen) and Rocco (Fidelio) in 2000, age 36, Gurnemanz (Parsifal) in 2003, age 39, Leporello (Don Giovanni) and King Marke in 2004, age 40, Méphistophélès in Gounod's Faust in 2005, age 41, Boris Godunov in 2010, age 46. He had his first solo recital in Carnegie Hall on 25 April 2009, age 44.6, where he sang German lieder from Schubert, Hugo Wolf and Schumann. Pape had his debut at London's Royal Opera Covent Garden as King Heinrich in Lohengrin in 1997, age 33; at the Opéra National de Paris under James Conlon as King Marke in Tristan in 1998, age 34; and at the Lyric Opera of Chicago under Christian Thielemann as Die Meistersinger's Pogner in 1999, age 35. His repertoire includes virtually all the great German bass roles, such as Mozart's Figaro, Leporello, and Don Giovanni, Pogner in Wagner's Die Meistersinger, as well as Ramfis in Aida, Filippo II in Don Carlo, Méphistophélès in Faust, Escamillo in Carmen, Gremin in Eugene Oneguine, and the title role of Boris Godunov.

Pape performs regularly in major opera houses, concert halls, and symphony orchestras around the world, as well as opera festivals such as Bayreuth, Glyndebourne, Lucerne, Orange, Saint-Petersburg, Salzburg, Verbier and White Nights.

Pape, 42, made his film debut as Sarastro in Kenneth Branagh's The Magic Flute, which premiered simultaneously at the 2006 Toronto International Film Festival, and the 2006 Venice Film Festival. He has a large discography.

Anna Netrebko: born 1971 (now 47)

1971 – 18 September - **Anna Yuryevna Netrebko** was born on 18 September 1971 (now (May 2019) age 47.6). She is a Russian operatic soprano, and holds dual Russian and Austrian citizenships, residing in Vienna, Austria, and in New York City. She is a frequent guest of the Metropolitan Opera, La Scala, Vienna State Opera, Mariinsky Theatre, and Royal Opera House in London. She was a student at the Saint Petersburg Conservatory, in Russia.

Netrebko made her operatic stage debut at the Mariinsky at age 22, in 1993, as Susanna in Le nozze di Figaro by Mozart. She went on to sing many prominent roles with the company, including Amina in La sonnambula, Pamina in Die Zauberflöte, Rosina in Il Barbiere di Siviglia, and Lucia in Lucia di Lammermoor. In 1994, she, 23, sang the Queen of the Night in Die Zauberflöte with the Riga Independent Opera Avangarda Akadēmija under conductor David Milnes. In 1995, at the age of 24, Netrebko made her American debut as Lyudmila in Glinka's Ruslan and Lyudmila, at the San Francisco Opera. Following this successful performance, she became a frequent guest singer in San Francisco. She is known as an acclaimed interpreter of other Russian operatic roles, such as Natasha in Prokofiev's War and Peace. Netrebko has also made successful roles into bel canto and romantic roles such as Gilda in Rigoletto, Mimì in La bohème, Giulietta in Bellini's I Capuleti e i Montecchi, and Elvira in I puritani.

In 2002, Netrebko, 31, made her debut at the Metropolitan Opera as Natasha in the Met premiere of War and Peace. In the same year, she sang her first Donna Anna at the Salzburg Festival's production of Don Giovanni, conducted by Nikolaus Harnoncourt. In 2003, Netrebko, 32, performed as Violetta in Verdi's La Traviata in Munich, the title role in Lucia di Lammermoor at the Los Angeles Opera, and Donna Anna at the Royal Opera House, Covent Garden. Her second album, Sempre Libera, was released the following year. She later appeared as Violetta Valéry in La Traviata at the Salzburg Festival, conducted by Carlo Rizzi, and in 2008 she, 37, performed the same role at Covent Garden to triumphant acclaim on the opening night. She, 33, sang Violetta's aria Sempre libera when she briefly played herself in the 2004 film The Princess Diaries 2: Royal

Engagement. In May 2008, she, 36.6, made her debut at the Paris Opera in I Capuleti e i Montecchi. In October and November 2010, she, 39, sang the role of Norina in Don Pasquale at New York's Metropolitan Opera House under conductor James Levine. The matinee performance on 13 November was broadcast nationwide by PBS. On 2 April 2011, she, 39.6, sang the title role of Gaetano Donizetti's Anna Bolena at the Vienna State Opera for a sold-out premiere there, and the repeat performance, on 5 April 2011, was broadcast live to cinemas around the world. On 7 December 2011 she, 40.2, opened the new season at La Scala in Milan as Donna Anna in Don Giovanni. Netrebko had the distinction of being invited to appear in three consecutive opening night new productions at the Metropolitan Opera: Anna Bolena in 2011 (age 40), L'elisir d'amore in 2012 (age 41), and Eugene Onegin in 2013 (age 42). She made several role debuts in 2017, including the title role of Adriana Lecouvreur at Mariinsky Theatre in June (age 45.7, the title role of Aida at Salzburg Festival in August (age 45.8), and Maddalena in Andrea Chénier at La Scala in December (age 46.2). In 2018, she debuted as Tosca at the Metropolitan Opera in April (age 46.6), and performed at the Summer Night Concert Schönbrunn in June. Netrebko has a child, and is married. She has many recordings.

Yonghoon Lee: born 1973 (now 46)

1973 - **Yonghoon Lee** was born (now (2019) age 46). He is a South Korean operatic tenor. Lee studied music at Seoul National University and The New School. He made his international debut in the title role of Don Carlo, at the Teatro Municipal in Santiago, Chile. He made his debut at the Metropolitan Opera in November 2010 (age 37) in the same role. In 2015, Lee, 42, made a complete opera video recording of Il Trovatore by Verdi, as Manrico, with Anna Netrebko, 44, as Leonora, at Metropolitan Opera.

Luca Pisaroni: born 1975 (now 44)

1975 - **Luca Pisaroni** was born in 1975 (now (2019) age 44). He is an Italian operatic bass-baritone, known for his roles in

Mozart's operas, but also the Baroque, as well as Rossini. Pisaroni's family moved to Busseto in Italy – the home of Giuseppe Verdi — when he was four years old. He began his training at the Conservatorio Giuseppe Verdi in Milan. Pisaroni's professional operatic debut was in the title role of Mozart's Le Nozze di Figaro in Klagenfurt, in 2001, age 26. Pisaroni, 27, sang Masetto at the 2002 Salzburg Festival in Mozart's Don Giovanni. Pisaroni has since appeared in major opera houses and festivals across Europe and America. In 2002, he, 27, debuted at the Whitsun Baroque Festival with Haydn's Nelson Mass, and at the Salzburg Summer Festival as Masetto in Don Giovanni, where he has performed every summer since. He sang Caliban in the baroque pasticcio The Enchanted Island at the Met in 2011, age 36, and he returned there in April/May 2014, age 39, for performances in La Cenerentola. He returned to the Met in 2015, age 40, as Leporello in the company's production of Don Giovanni. It was through his 2002, age 27, appearance in Salzburg that Pisaroni met both the American baritone Thomas Hampson (who was singing the Don) and his daughter Cate. Cate and Pisaroni were subsequently married and now make their home in Vienna.

Elīna Garanča: born 1976 (now 42)

1976 – 16 September - **Elīna Garanča** was born on 16 September 1976 (now (May 2019) age 42.6)). She is a Latvian mezzo-soprano, and began to study singing in her hometown of Riga in 1996, then continued her studies in Vienna and in the United States. By 1999 she, 23, had won first place in a significant competition in Finland, and had begun a career in Europe. She entered the Latvian Academy of Music in 1996, age 20, to study singing with Sergej Martinov, then continued her studies in Vienna with Irina Gavrilovici, and in the United States with Virginia Zeani. Garanča began her professional career at the Meiningen Court Theatre, Meiningen, Germany, and later worked at the Frankfurt Opera. Garanča's international breakthrough came in 2003 at the Salzburger Festspiele, when she, 27, sang Annio in a production of Mozart's La Clemenza di Tito, conducted by Nikolaus Harnoncourt. Major engagements followed quickly, such as Charlotte in Werther,

Dorabella in Così fan tutte at the Vienna State Opera (2004, age 28) and Dorabella in a Paris production directed by Patrice Chéreau (2005, age 29). In 2006, she, 30, returned to La Clemenza di Tito, this time singing the part of Sesto. On 12 January 2008, Garanča, 31.3, made her debut at the Metropolitan Opera in New York, in the role of Rosina in Rossini's Il Barbiere di Siviglia. Garanča, 34, sang the leading role of Georges Bizet's Carmen in the 2010 production of the Metropolitan Opera. In May 2018, Garanča, 41.6, made her stage role debut as Dalila in Camille Saint-Saëns' Samson et Dalila at Wiener Staatsoper conducted by Marco Armiliato. Garanča is married to the conductor Karel Mark Chichon, and they have two daughters.

Japan, Chiba Newtown (35 km northeast of Tokyo Imperial Palace, 24 km west of Narita Airport), Alcazar Theater (200 m northeast of Chiba Newtown Chuo Station on Hokuso Line).

Yukiko Aragaki: born 1979 (now 40)

1979 – **Yukiko Aragaki** was born in Tokyo in 1979 (now 40). She is a Japanese soprano, studied at the Tokyo University of the Arts, obtaining her bachelor's degree in classical voice, and her master's degree in opera. She is the winner of a many vocal competitions in Japan. Aragaki debuted as Susanna in The Marriage of Figaro (Le Nozze di Figaro) under the baton of Hanns Martin Schneidt in Tokyo, as well as in numerous other roles in Japan, including: Adina (The Elixir of Love / L'Elisir d'Amore), Giulietta (The Capulets and the Montagues / I Capuleti e i Montecchi), Carolina (The Secret Marriage / Il Matrimonio Segreto). She sings in Gianni Schicchi at the New National Theatre in Tokyo, and, following her graduation, interprets Gretel (Hansel and Gretel / Hänsel und Gretel). Having been awarded the prestigious annual "Artist Abroad" scholarship by the Government of Japan, Aragaki, 29, travels to Italy in 2008. There she is admitted to the Opera Studio of the Accademia Santa Cecilia in Rome to work under Renata Scotto, and becomes a member of the Young Artists Programme at the Teatro dell'Opera di Roma. Aragaki decided to settle in Italy, and continues her vocal studies under the guidance of Mariella Devia, and Janet Perry. Aragaki was Zerlina in Mozart's Don Giovanni at the Teatro Consorziale in Budrio (Bo). She debuts as Liu in Turandot under Gianluigi Gelmetti in Tokyo, sings Egmont (Beethoven) under Hubert Soudant at the Tokyo Symphony Orchestra's Summer Festival, as well as Musetta (La Bohème). In 2012, she, 33, interprets Sofia in Il Signor Bruschino (Rossini) at the Piccolo Festival in Udine, and the following year is engaged to perform Susanna (The Marriage of Figaro / Le Nozze di Figaro) at the Nissey Theater in Tokyo, as well as Frasquita (Carmen) under Donato Renzetti at the Teatro Verdi in Trieste. In Tokyo, she sings Beethoven's Ninth Symphony, and then performs with the Tokyo Symphony Orchestra as the soloist of a Mozart concert in Opera City, as well as in Peer Gynt (Grieg). In 2015, she, 36, sings Gilda (Rigoletto) under Andrea Battistoni in Tokyo, in a co-production with the Teatro Regio of Parma, then performs Elvira in Gazzaniga's Don Giovanni at the Teatro Verdi in Pisa.

In 2016, Aragaki, 37, was Pamina (The Magic Flute / Die Zauberflöte) at the Teatro Goldoni in Livorno, at the Teatro Verdi in Pisa, and at the Teatro Giglio in Lucca. In 2018, she, 39, sings Lauretta (Gianni Schicchi) and Sister Genovieffa (Sister Angelica / Suor Angelica) from Puccini's Tryptich (Il Trittico) at the New National Theater of Tokyo, in a production by D. Micheletto, conducted by B. De Billy.

1983 - With the introduction of noise-free compact discs, the vinyl record begins a steep decline.

1988 - CDs outsell vinyl records for the first time.

1990 - Compact discs surpass cassette tapes as the preferred medium for recorded music.

2003 – Recent rediscoveries of works by Vivaldi: two psalm settings of *Nisi Dominus* (RV 803, in eight movements).

2005 – *Dixit Dominus* (RV 807, in eleven movements).

2006 – Vivaldi's 1730 opera *Argippo* (RV 697), which had been considered lost, was rediscovered by the harpsichordist and conductor Ondřej Macek.

2008 – 3 May - Ondřej Macek and his Hofmusici orchestra performed Vivaldi's opera *Argippo* (RV 697) at Prague Castle — its first performance in 278 years, since 1730.

2013 – 10 October - the bicentenary of Verdi's birth was widely celebrated in broadcasts and performances.

Vinyl records continue to make a strong comeback. While CD sales decline 14.5% and digital sales decline 2%, vinyl sales increase 33.5% for the year.

USA, San Francisco (1776, on the north tip of a peninsula, near the Pacific Ocean (west) and San Francisco Bay (east)), the northeast part of the Golden Gate Park (1870, 4.1 km^2), the bronze and stone sculpture (1916) Miguel de Cervantes (1547 – 1616) Memorial, with Don Quijote (right down) and Sancho Panza (left down), by Jo Mora (1876 – 1947). In 1605 Cervantes publishes first part of The Ingenious Gentleman Don Quijote of La Mancha, second part in 1615. Cervantes is the father of the modern novel, and his book is one of the most widely read and translated books in the world.

Bibliography

"The Histories" by Polybius
"Discours de la Méthode" by René Descartes
"Meditationes de prima philosophia" by René Descartes
"Philosophiae Naturalis Principia Mathematica" by Isaac Newton
Chinese encyclopedia Gujin Tushu Jicheng (Imperial Enciclopaedia)
"Encyclopédie" by Jean-Baptiste le Rond d'Alembert and Denis Diderot
"Encyclopaedia Britannica" by over 4,400 contributors
"Encyclopedia Americana" by Francis Lieber
"Grand Larousse encyclopédique en 24 volumes" by Albert Ducrocq
Nobel Prize Organization
"The Cambridge History of Medicine", edited by Roy Porter
"Great Russian Encyclopedia" by Yury Osipov
"Encyclopedia of China"
"Enciclopedia Italiana di Scienze, Lettere ed Arti" (35 volume), by Giovanni Treccani
Concise Oxford Dictionary of Opera
"Allgemeine Encyclopädie der Wissenschaften und Künste" by Johann Samuel Ersch und Johann Gottfried Gruber
Grove Dictionary of Music and Musicians
"Gran Enciclopedia de España"

Michael M. Dediu is also the author of these books (which can be found on Amazon.com):

1. Aphorisms and quotations – with examples and explanations
2. Axioms, aphorisms and quotations – with examples and explanations
3. 100 Great Personalities and their Quotations
4. Professor Petre P. Teodorescu – A Great Mathematician and Engineer
5. Professor Ioan Goia – A Dedicated Engineering Professor

6. Venice (Venezia) – a new perspective. A short presentation with photographs
7. La Serenissima (Venice) - a new photographic perspective. A short presentation with many photos
8. Grand Canal – Venice. A new photographic viewpoint. A short presentation with many photos
9. Piazza San Marco – Venice. A different photographic view. A short presentation with many photos
10. Roma (Rome) - La Città Eterna. A new photographic view. A short presentation with many photos
11. Why is Rome so Fascinating? A short presentation with many photos
12. Rome, Boston and Helsinki. A short photographic presentation
13. Rome and Tokyo – two captivating cities. A short photographic presentation
14. Beautiful Places on Earth – A new photographic presentation
15. From Niagara Falls to Mount Fuji via Rome - A novel photographic presentation
16. From the USA and Canada to Italy and Japan - A fresh photographic presentation
17. Paris – Why So Many Call This City Mon Amour - A lovely photographic presentation
18. The City of Light – Paris (La Ville-Lumière) - A kaleidoscopic photographic presentation
19. Paris (Lutetia Parisiorum) – the romance capital of the world - A kaleidoscopic photographic view
20. Paris and Tokyo – a joyful photographic presentation. With a preamble about the Universe
21. From USA to Japan via Canada – A cheerful photographic documentary
22. 200 Wonderful Places, In The Last 50 Years – A personal photographic documentary
23. Must see places in USA and Japan - A kaleidoscopic photographic documentary
24. Grandeurs of the World - A kaleidoscopic photographic documentary
25. Corneliu Leu – writer on the same wavelength as Mark Twain. An American viewpoint

26. From Berkeley to Pompeii via Rome – A kaleidoscopic photographic documentary
27. From America to Europe via Japan - A kaleidoscopic photographic documentary
28. Discover America and Japan - A photographic documentary
29. J. R. Lucas – philosopher on a creative parallel with Plato, An American viewpoint
30. From America to Switzerland via France - A photographic documentary
31. From Bretton Woods to New York via Cape Cod - A photographic documentary
32. Splendid Places on the Atlantic Coast of the U. S. A. - A photographic documentary
33. Fourteen nice Cities on three Continents - A photographic documentary
34. 17 Picturesque Cities on the World Map - A photographic documentary
35. Unforgettable Places from Four Continents including Trump buildings - A photographic documentary
36. Dediu Newsletter, Volume 1, Number 1, 6 December 2016 – Monthly news, review, comments and suggestions for a better and wiser world
37. Dediu Newsletter, Volume 1, Number 2, 6 January 2017 (available at www.derc.com).
38. Dediu Newsletter, Volume 1, Number 3, 6 February 2017 (available at www.derc.com).
39. London and Greenwich, A photographic documentary
40. Dediu Newsletter, Volume 1, Number 4, 6 March 2017 (available also at www.derc.com).
41. Dediu Newsletter, Volume 1, Number 5, 6 April 2017 (available also at www.derc.com).
42. Dediu Newsletter, Volume 1, Number 6, 6 May 2017 (available also at www.derc.com).
43. Dediu Newsletter, Volume 1, Number 7, 6 June 2017 (available also at www.derc.com).
44. London, Oxford and Cambridge, A photographic documentary
45. Dediu Newsletter, Volume 1, Number 8, 6 July 2017 (available also at www.derc.com).

46. Dediu Newsletter, Volume 1, Number 9, 6 August 2017 (available also at www.derc.com).
47. Dediu Newsletter, Volume 1, Number 10, 6 September 2017 (available also at www.derc.com).
48. Three Great Professors: President Woodrow Wilson, Historian Germán Arciniegas, Mathematician Gheorghe Vrănceanu, A chronological and photographic documentary
49. Dediu Newsletter, Volume 1, Number 11, 6 October 2017 (available also at www.derc.com).
50 Dediu Newsletter, Volume 1, Number 12, 6 November 2017 (available also at www.derc.com).
51 Dediu Newsletter, Volume 2, Number 1 (13), 6 December 2017 (available also at www.derc.com).
52 Two Great Leaders: Augustus and George Washington, A chronological and photographic documentary
53. Dediu Newsletter, Volume 2, Number 2 (14), 6 January 2018 (available also at www.derc.com).
54. Newton, Benjamin Franklin, and Gauss, A chronological and photographic documentary
55. Dediu Newsletter, Volume 2, Number 3 (15), 6 February 2018 (available also at www.derc.com).
56. 2017: World Top Events, But Many Little Known, A chronological and photographic documentary
57. Dediu Newsletter, Volume 2, Number 4 (16), 6 March 2018 (available also at www.derc.com).
58. Vergilius, Horatius, Ovidius, and Shakespeare, A chronological and photographic documentary.
59. Dediu Newsletter, Volume 2, Number 5 (17), 6 April 2018 (available also at www.derc.com).
60. Dediu Newsletter, Volume 2, Number 6 (18), 6 May 2018 (available also at www.derc.com).
61. Vivaldi, Bach, Mozart, and Verdi, A chronological and photographic documentary
62. Dediu Newsletter, Volume 2, Number 7 (19), 6 June 2018 (available also at www.derc.com).
63. Dediu Newsletter, Volume 2, Number 8 (20), 6 July 2018 (available also at www.derc.com).
64. Dediu Newsletter, Volume 2, Number 9 (21), 6 August 2018 (available also at www.derc.com).

65. World History, a new perspective - A chronological and photographic documentary.
66. World Humor History with over 100 Jokes, a new perspective - A chronological and photographic documentary
67. Dediu Newsletter, Vol 2, N 10 (22), 6 September 2018
68. Dediu Newsletter, Vol 2, N 11 (23), 6 October 2018
69. Da Vinci, Michelangelo, Rembrandt, Rodin - A chronological and photographic documentary
70. Dediu Newsletter, Vol 2, N 12 (24), 6 November 2018
71. Dediu Newsletter, Vol 3, N 1 (25), 6 December 2018
72. From Euclid to Edison - revelries in the last 75 years - A chronological and photographic documentary
73. Dediu Newsletter, Vol 3, N 2 (26), 6 January 2019
74. Socrates to Churchill - Aphorisms celebrated after 1960 - A chronological and photographic documentary
75. Dediu Newsletter Vol 3, Number 3 (27), 6 February 2019
76. Hippocrates to Fleming: Medicine History celebrated after 1943 - A chronological and photographic documentary
77. Dediu Newsletter, Volume 3, Number 4 (28), 6 March 2019
78. Dediu Newsletter, Volume 3, Number 5 (29), 6 April 2019
79. Archimedes to Ford: Invention History celebrated after 1943 - A chronological and photographic documentary
80. Dediu Newsletter, Volume 3, Number 6 (30), 6 May 2019

Michael M. Dediu is the editor of these books (also on Amazon.com):

1. Sophia Dediu: The life and its torrents – Ana. In Europe around 1920
2. Proceedings of the 4th International Conference "Advanced Composite Materials Engineering" COMAT 2012
3. Adolf Shvedchikov: I am an eternal child of spring – poems in English, Italian, French, German, Spanish and Russian
4. Adolf Shvedchikov: Life's Enigma – poems in English, Italian and Russian
5. Adolf Shvedchikov: Everyone wants to be HAPPY – poems in English, Spanish and Russian
6. Adolf Shvedchikov: My Life, My Love – poems in English, Italian and Russian
7. Adolf Shvedchikov: I am the gardener of love – poems in English and Russian
8. Adolf Shvedchikov: Amaretta di Saronno – poems in English and Russian
9. Adolf Shvedchikov: A Russian Rediscovers America
10. Adolf Shvedchikov: Parade of Life - poems in English and Russian
11. Adolf Shvedchikov: Overcoming Sorrow - poems in English and Russian
12. Sophia Dediu: Sophia meets Japan
13. Corneliu Leu: Roosevelt, Churchill, Stalin and Hitler: Their surprising role in Eastern Europe in 1944
14. Proceedings of the 5th International Conference "Computational Mechanics and Virtual Engineering" COMEC 2013
15. Georgeta Simion – Potanga: Beyond Imagination: A Thought-provoking novel inspired from mid-20th century events
16. Ana Dediu: The poetry of my life in Europe and The USA
17. Ana Dediu: The Four Graces
18. Proceedings of the 5th International Conference "Advanced Composite Materials Engineering" COMAT 2014
19. Sophia Dediu: Chocolate Cook Book: Is there such a thing as too much chocolate?

20. Sorin Vlase: Mechanical Identifiability in Automotive Engineering
21. Gabriel Dima: The Evolution of the Aerostructures – Concept and Technologies
22. Proceedings of the 6th International Conference "Computational Mechanics and Virtual Engineering" COMEC 2015
23. Sophia Dediu: Cook Book 1 A-B-C Common sense cooking
24. Sophia Dediu: Dim Sum Spring Festival
25. Ana Dediu and Sophia Dediu: Europe in 1985: A chronological and photographic documentary
26 Stefan Staretu: Europe: Serbian Despotate of Srem and the Romanian area. Between the 14th and the 16th Centuries

Italy, Rome (753 BC), on the west side of Piazza del Popolo (1822), Fontana del Nettuno (1823, by Giovanni Ceccarini, showing Neptune with his Trident and two Tritons (left and right)).